THE SIX-DAY STORY:

HOW TO WRITE A NOVEL IN LESS THAN A WEEK, AND OTHER THINGS I'VE LEARNT

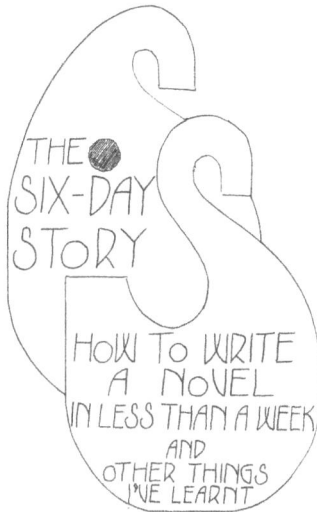

THE
SIX-DAY
STORY

HOW TO WRITE
A NOVEL
IN LESS THAN A WEEK
AND
OTHER THINGS
I'VE LEARNT

About the author

Sass Wilson lives in the north-west of Britain and has three grown-up children.

In the six days leading up to her 50th birthday, she set herself an exercise – to write a book in a week.

The Six-Day Story describes the process of writing a novel in a week, what led up to it, what came after, and what was learnt in the process.

The product of the book-in-a-week exercise is called *Tenderfield* and is published alongside *The Six-Day Story*.

Find out more from: www.gladhouse.co.uk.

THE SIX-DAY STORY

HOW TO WRITE A NOVEL IN LESS THAN A WEEK, AND OTHER THINGS I'VE LEARNT

Sass Wilson

The Six-Day Story: how to write a novel in less than a week, and other things I've learnt.

Copyright © Sass Wilson 2016

First published in 2016 by
Gladhouse Press (GhP)
Preston, Lancashire, United Kingdom.

A catalogue record for this book is available
from the British Library.

ISBN 978-0-9935604-1-5

Typeset by Carnegie Book Production, Lancaster.

Cover design by Frankie Saundry.

Printed by Jellyfish Solutions

Gladhouse

Making makes the ordinary extraordinary

"Let's call her Glad because we're glad to have her." So our family myth has it that, at the age of four, my dad Harry Wilson named his baby sister, my Aunty Glad. Nearly ninety years later, Aunty Glad's legacy has allowed me to invest in Gladhouse, a series of personal projects designed to increase gladness (joy and gratitude combined). Gladhouse celebrates making things, recycling, art and craft, amateurism, having a go, giving life a try, the artist as experimenter, quiet productivity, the therapeutic nature of creating things using our hands, eyes and minds, and spreading the word by example rather than lecture.

Gladhouse Press (GhP)

I have set up Gladhouse Press to publish books written by my family and friends. By bringing our stories into print we are transforming what could be seen as something ordinary into something extraordinary.

I hope what we are doing inspires and encourages other people to write, draw and make things because by making things we are turning the ordinary into the extraordinary – that is what human beings can do so well.

Gladhouse Press is a not-for-profit organisation. Buying this book will enable us to produce more books in the future. Thank you for your support.

GLADHOUSE PRESS

Thanks, apologies
and making amends

I was once told that it is not good for us to apologise too much – perhaps it is best to say sorry only when it is truly meant and felt, when it is relevant.

For a while I took this advice to heart and, rather than constantly apologising for being late (I am a late person by nature), instead I thanked my family, friends and colleagues for their patience waiting for me to turn up; I was grateful for them knowing me well and understanding how I just had a lot to fit in to my time.

Turning 'sorry' into 'thank you' made me aware of how apologies and gratitude can be linked. It is to do with lack and gain, I think. When I say thank you, when I am grateful, it is because I feel I have gained something. When I say sorry, it is because I feel you have lost something. If I am truly sorry, and feel that I am responsible for your loss, then I would like to try and make amends – I would like to try and pay something back.

I am grateful for everything I have experienced that has enabled me to learn so much and thereby produce this book.

Unfortunately, my learning process was sometimes at the expense of others. There is much that I am not proud of in my past, and while saying sorry to those I have hurt and wronged, I would also like to say thank you – thank you for the opportunity to learn about the world, and about people and about relationships. I learnt some lessons the hard way. I was not always kind. At the time, I was struggling and was not able to see a way to be a better me. In honour of all that I have learnt, I now try to make amends by being a better me every day. I am not always able to pay back the people from whom I have gained, nor am I able to make restitution to the people I have wronged, so instead I shall try to pay forward – putting into the world a better example of how to live, a version of me that lives well, gives more and takes less.

I am grateful for the opportunity to do this.

Thank you all my friends, past and present, for your love and encouragement. Thank you everyone with whom I have come into contact, particularly over the past 12 years while I have been working towards the better version of me – some of you I may have only met in passing, but you have all touched my spirit and I have gained from you. For that I am very glad. Thank you to the men who have put up with me in relationships – there was as much delight as sorrow for me, and I hope there was for you too. Thank you to the therapists who listened so well, in particular thank you Kim and Steve. Thank you to the inspirers and encouragers, particularly my fellow students on counselling courses. Thank you to my longstanding women friends, who have been the power behind me in troubled times – Diane, Jae, Judy, and Helen, you were there on the ground when it really counted. You have loved me when I was behaving in unloveable ways. Thank you Lesley, Ade, Beanie and Bod – you were there as my precious pals at a distance. Thank you to all my friends – new and old – you have patiently put up with me being unavailable for brews and chats while I've been writing and making this book. Thank you to the writing group for keeping me writing, and for the friendships to come out of it. Thank you to the strong women teachers, mentors and managers: you may no longer be around but you continue to inspire me – Christine, Lee, Liz and Bernadette, Dorothy, Anna, and Linda. Thank you Mum, for helping me produce this book, and for enduring my worst traits – I know I put you through a lot. In my life every day, I am most grateful for my children, who entertain, amaze, and impress me with their wit, style and wisdom. Our joint journey has not always been easy – kids, I know you understand that I have not meant to get things wrong but sometimes I have – I am so sorry for that and at the same time so grateful for your understanding.

This is where thank you meets sorry.

Dedication

For Mum, for being so lovely, always.

CONTENTS

INTRODUCTION – THE IDEA   1

  1. The Six-Day Story   1
  2. What Is Different About This Book?   2
  3. So What's This Book About Then?   7

PART ONE – PREPARING (SETTING THE SCENE)   11

  1. I Am Not A Writer   11
  2. Faith   14
  3. Being The Person I Want To Be   21
  4. Being An Amateur – Doing It For
      Love (Not Money)   26
  5. Do What You Love, And Love
      What You Do   36
  6. Mapping What Works   47
  7. The SE3R Storyboard   51
  8. Completion – A Perfectionist in
      Recovery   54

PART TWO – MAKING AND DOING
(WHAT ACTUALLY HAPPENED)   63

  1. The Build-Up   63
  2. Third Time Lucky   76
  3. The Countdown and
      The Word Count   80
  4. Beginning to Plot   86
  5. Writing by Numbers   92
  6. Six Days   101
  7. The Statistics   112

PART THREE – LEARNING (FROM DOING)   122

   1. The Knowledge   125
   2. The Motivation   132
   3. Flexibility   140
   4. Purpose   145
   5. Getting Told v. Being Offered   161
   6. That's Your Opinion   169
   7. What Works?   172
   8. Focus   177
   9. Limits, Pressure and Priorities   185
   10. Laziness v. Self-Control   193
   11. Routine and Habits   199
   12. A Little Bit About Writing   206

PART FOUR – DOING IT AGAIN
(STARTING TO PLAN THE NEXT BOOK/S)   220

   1. Planning The Next Story   223
   2. The Importance of Coherence   234
   3. Notes to Self   239
   4. Trying Again   246

CONCLUSION   250

   1. Choice   250
   2. Making the Point   256
   3. Who Have I Written This Book
      For?   260

APPENDIX I – MY RECIPE CARD FOR
WRITING A BOOK IN A WEEK   265

APPENDIX II – YOUR RECIPE CARD FOR
WRITING A BOOK IN A WEEK   268

AFTER WORDS   269

REFERENCES AND RESOURCES   275

INTRODUCTION -
THE IDEA

The Six-Day Story

Last year I wrote a story in six days.

I hesitate to call it a novel because it's more of an action story than a work of literature, but it is novel-sized: it is over 60,000 words long.

So I'm going to force myself to write this down:

Last November I wrote a novel in six days

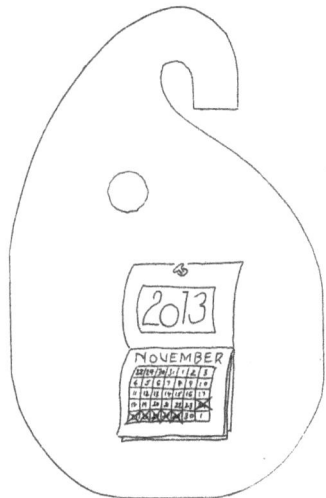

There. I've gone and said it now. I feel a bit nervous putting it out there, saying the words, but I feel a bit brave too.

I wanted to prove I could write a book in a week. I wanted to prove it could be done. So I did it.

I wrote a novel in less than a week.

This book tells the story of how I did that.

And what I learnt.

What Is Different About This Book?

If you have picked up this book, chances are you may have looked at other books about writing and about writing whole books.

You may want to know: what's so different about this book?

Why invest time, money and energy in this book and not in the other books on the subject?

Well, for a start, I'm not saying don't invest in the other books – in fact, as I write this I am sure I will recommend other books, there are some great ones out there and only by trying them will you find out which ones work best for you.

But what you want to know is: how is this book different to the others?

I'll tell you how.

Firstly, I wrote it.

And that doesn't mean it's brilliant. Of course not. In fact, quite the opposite, it probably has many flaws. But it does mean it is written by a person, not a professional writer. (More about this later.) And it is written by someone who has recently tried to write a whole book in a week – and succeeded.

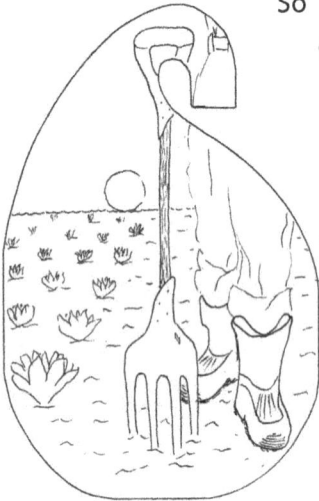

So it is fresh. Organic. Not grown in a greenhouse, but out in the real muddy allotment of have-a-go self-teaching. No pesticides used. (This may mean you find metaphorical aphids in your verbal salad, but I've tried to pick out the metaphorical slugs at least.)

And secondly, it has illustrations.

Not just jokey little cartoons of weary writers slumped over typewriters, but other illustrations too, diagrams as well I hope. I'm going to make sure this book has as many pictures as I can cram into it. Or possibly as many pictures and diagrams as I am capable of drawing. Since I am only self-taught at drawing as well, this is going to be a bit of a challenge, but that's only a good thing, challenges are good for me...and I can always leave out the really bad drawings, it's not like I have to include everything I do.

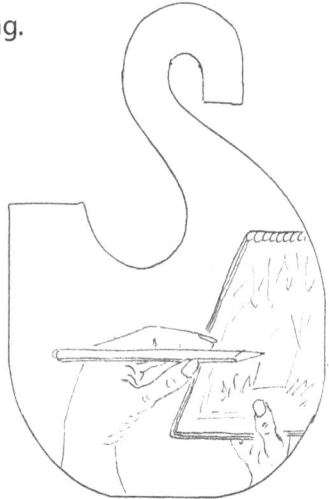

And thirdly, (and this is where I hesitate again because you might put the book down) I'm not going to tell you how to write. (I'm not sure I'm qualified to do so either...)

But I don't think I need to tell you how to write.

Perhaps you like writing, in which case you'll be doing it already.

Or perhaps you like reading, in which case I don't need to tell you how to write.

WARNING

THIS BOOK WILL NOT TEACH YOU HOW TO WRITE

Or perhaps you fancy having a go at writing a whole book.

Or maybe you just want to know what writing a whole book entails?

WRITE A NOVEL!

GO READER!

If any of those are true, you don't need me to tell you **how** to write. What you need me to do is to say: 'go on, have a go'.

So I won't tell you how to write. There are plenty of books and courses (and better qualified people) that can tell you how to write. Anyway, reading, writing, practising writing, sharing your writing, and getting feedback are the best ways to learn how to write, and, there, I've told you that now so we can get on with the rest of it.

So What's This Book About Then?

This book is about completion.

It is about getting something done, and getting that thing done in a timeframe. Quite a short timeframe actually.

It is about getting hold of a creative idea, gathering it from my mind like herbs from a meadow; then planning

what I would cook up; then the process I went through to bring that dish to the table.

Okay, so, to date, as I write now, I have only tried this dish (book) out on my family, but, by the time you read this, the book I wrote last year will have been read by a wider audience, possibly published, possibly even read by you.

I will tell you how I did it, how I wrote a novel in six days, and I'll think about what I learnt from doing it, and offer you the ideas I come up with.

Getting things done (and not getting things done) and the struggle to get things done are subjects I am more than qualified to write a book on. I may have limited experience of writing novels, but I have a

lifetime's experience of not getting through my TO DO list.

If my life were a classical drama with myself as the valiant human hero, the underdog, then the capricious gods who throw insurmountable obstacles in my way would include Procrastinata, the god of putting off difficult things to another time.

"Oh, but it's easy for you," you might say, "look, you're a writer, that's how you can write a book in a week."

But, as I've already told you, I'm not a writer, or at least I wasn't when I started.

9

And that is where I'll begin.

PART ONE – PREPARING (SETTING THE SCENE)

I Am Not A Writer

"But you are!" I hear you cry. "Look, you have written this book, I have it in my hands, you have written it, I am reading it!"

Well, that's true, of course. I have written this book, and I did write a novel in less than a week. But I'm not a Writer. You know, not a *writer*. I may write things, I write, yes, but I don't think of myself as a writer.

TORTURED WRITER SUFFERING IN A GARRET

ME GOING SHOPPING

Because I'm not a professional writer.

Because I don't do it all the time.

Because I'm not trained, or taught, or qualified, or experienced.

I just like writing, so I write.

The first point I'm trying to make is that I am not so different to yourself.

I am more like all the people in the world who *don't* think they are writers,
than I am like the people who *do* think they are writers.

I can feel a diagram coming on...

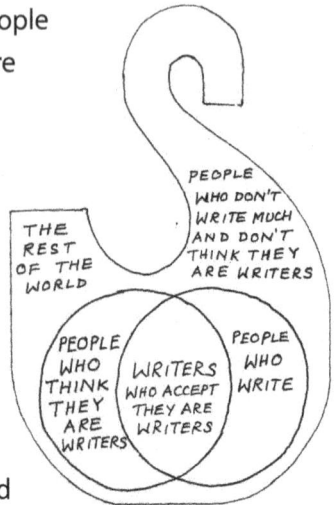

And the second point I want to make is that people (you and

me) who don't think of themselves as writers can write, and do write, books.

Now that doesn't mean the books we write are great literature. And it doesn't mean that they are necessarily very good books (they may be good, but on the other hand they may not); and it doesn't mean that anyone beyond our friends and family will want to read our books necessarily.

But don't think you can't write a book just because you're not a *Writer*.

You can, because I did.

And then, a bit like magic, when you've written it...you do (kind of) become a writer. (Even if you still don't feel like one.)

HEY PRESTO!

WE WRITE ⟹ WRITERS

Faith

Once, a long time ago, before my children were born, I worked in a small office in a converted mill building. A couple of offices down the corridor there was a small PR company, owned by a couple who thought of themselves as professional writers, because they wrote press releases for a living. I became very good friends with a woman who worked alongside them as their assistant (she is still one of my dearest friends); we would spend our lunch-breaks together and chat about our work, and our bosses.

One day my friend came to me and asked me to write something for her, I can't remember what it was, a letter maybe, perhaps an application letter for a new job. I can remember being surprised though. My friend was bright and creative, intelligent and talkative, why did she want me to write this letter for her? She wanted me to write it for her because she thought she wasn't much good at writing.

"What do you want to say?" I asked her.

She told me what she wanted to say.

She said it out loud. It was fine. It said what she wanted to say.

"So write that," I said.

"Really?" she said.

"Yes," said I.

It really was as simple as that. Writing often is, isn't it? The trouble is that people don't *believe* it can be that simple. They think writing is something special. At that time, my friend had spent a good number of years working alongside two people who made out that writing was something special, something that only certain trained or clever people could do; they made it into a mystery, like some lawyers try to make the law incomprehensible for people without law degrees. So my friend thought she couldn't write. She didn't *believe* she could do it. Once she found she could do it, once she believed she could, there was no stopping her – she went on to do a degree, she got a great job and became a manager and an expert in her field. I bet she writes every day now and doesn't think anything of it.

CONTENTS OF THIS BOX INCOMPREHENSIBLE IF YOU DON'T KNOW THE CODE

TOP SECRET

One of the things about faith is that it can be grown.

The best way to grow faith is to do the thing we want to do – then, when we look round and catch ourselves doing it, then we can **see** we can do that thing. And if we do this over and over again, day after day, then we end up really **feeling** we can do that thing.

FLOWERS OF FAITH

It is as if we grow the feeling of belief in ourselves by watering it with actions, by feeding it with proof.

If we want to extend the metaphor, then possibly love and approval might be like the light and warmth from sunlight. I do believe, however, that we can generate

ACTIONS AND PROOF

love and approval for ourselves from within – perhaps this is like an artificial daylight bulb.

So if we want to grow a belief that we can write, then by doing it every day we will grow faith in ourselves.

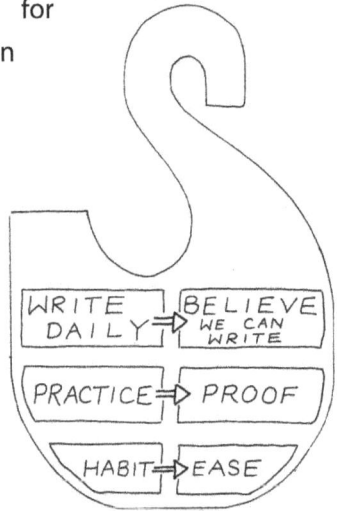

WRITE DAILY ⇒ BELIEVE WE CAN WRITE

PRACTICE ⇒ PROOF

HABIT ⇒ EASE

Once upon a time I used to think I couldn't run. My mum had an amusing (?) anecdote about me: I was a teenager, a young goth, in the 1980s, we were out in town and we were late as usual, we were going to miss our bus. "Run, Sass, run!" my mum shouted. "But I don't know how!" I wailed back at her.

"BUT I DON'T KNOW HOW TO RUN!"

BUS

I had been plump and quiet and studious at school, always picked last for teams in PE lessons, always in the slow chatty shivering group for cross-country. As a young adult, I was busy, practical and hard-working, but I was never sporty. As a child, my family had been arty, and sport just wasn't within our remit. I grew up feeling more like an eccentric individual than a team player. I was never one of the crowd.

In my thirties and forties, I started to go to the gym and to get a little fitter. It was therapeutic for me, beneficial for my emotional well-being as much as for my ageing body. Once I was a little fitter, I tried going for a run one day, just a few hundred yards up and down a lane, a side road where no one could see me. I got a taste for it. Running was something I could do on my own. I like things I can do on my own – I am more cat than dog.

CAT
sociable
sometimes

DOG
sociable
all the time

"I do what
I want"

"I do what
you want"

I discovered that I liked the freedom of running – just putting on some sweatpants and trainers and opening the front door, whatever time of day, whatever the weather, even if I was on holiday. I was never fast, but I loved it, and it probably only took a few weeks of daily practice to grow in me the belief that I could run.

Daily practice is important though. We only learnt to brush our teeth on autopilot because we did it every day as small children.

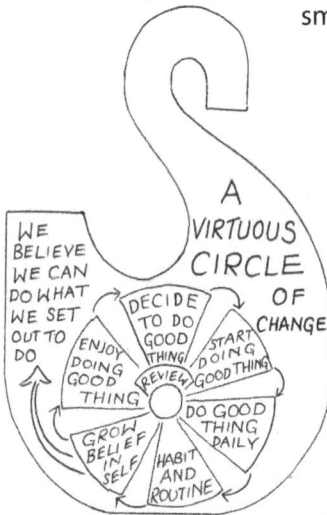

A VIRTUOUS CIRCLE OF CHANGE

WE BELIEVE WE CAN DO WHAT WE SET OUT TO DO

DECIDE TO DO GOOD THING

START DOING GOOD THING

ENJOY DOING GOOD THING

REVIEW GOOD THING

DO GOOD THING DAILY

HABIT AND ROUTINE

GROW BELIEF IN SELF

So, if we follow the example of me learning to run, then we will believe we can write when we are writing every day for a few weeks. Give it over a month…and then see how you feel. Maybe you'll feel you are beginning to be a writer.

Being The Person I Want To Be

Growing faith is a principle I've met some other significant times in my life.

It cropped up when I was researching addiction.

When it comes to combating addictive behaviour, the 'growing faith' principle can be seen in 'one day at a time' – each day that we are sober, we are proving to ourselves we can do it. Each day that we stick to our healthy eating plan, we are growing faith in ourselves.

We need to water the flower of faith on a regular basis.

Growing faith in ourselves can also be seen in the practice of acting 'as if'.

Even if I don't always feel great about myself, if I still act **as if** I am a valuable person, and if I do this over and over again, I will believe it more and more. Treating myself with care and affection, *as if* I were worthy of respect and love, I grow faith in myself that I am a loveable person.

This is certainly something I can see happened to me over the ten years it took me to re-find myself. Occasionally I did it deliberately: I obliged myself to treat myself well, to take care, to consider myself, to think what was in my own best interests. And sometimes it just happened, thanks to so many of my friends and family and colleagues thinking well of me even when I was struggling and not behaving well, not being the kind and thoughtful person I wanted to be.

I had a mini turning point, a moment of enlightenment, when I was at quite a low ebb. The light was switched on for me by a fellow student on a counselling course. I was in one of the counselling rooms at the college and my fellow student and I were taking it in turns to be the listener (pretend counsellor) and the talker (pretend counselling client). It was my turn to listen. Although my head was full of my own fretting and the issues in my life at that time, I managed successfully to turn down the volume of chatter in my head so that I was able to *feel* (hear and understand) what my fellow student was telling me. She had been through her own hard times in the recent past, but thanks to her own perseverance and generous nature, she found herself in a good place in her life at last. She was happy. The words she used to describe why and how she was happy have stayed with me: she said, "I like how I am with people now." I noticed the

"I like how I am with people now"

COUNSELLING SUITE 3

phrase when she said it, and repeated it back to her later in the session.

Almost immediately these words began to have an effect in my life. I wanted to like myself in the way that my fellow student now found she liked herself; I wanted that quality of happiness and peace. I wanted to 'like the way I was with people'. Little by little, the way I was with people changed. I was beginning to be the person I wanted to be. I wanted to be less bossy with the children – so when I was with them I made an effort to be the person I wanted to be. I wanted to listen more and talk less. I wanted to be less critical. I wanted to be less snappy with my mum, I didn't want to make her cry when I was irritable and stressed. I wanted to be accepting, kind, patient, humourous…the list went on and on. To begin with, it seemed out of reach, there seemed to be so many things I wanted to change about the way I interacted with people. But that moment with my fellow counselling student had shown me the way forward – the answer was to shift how I 'was' with people to something I liked. Then I could be happy as she was. Then there would

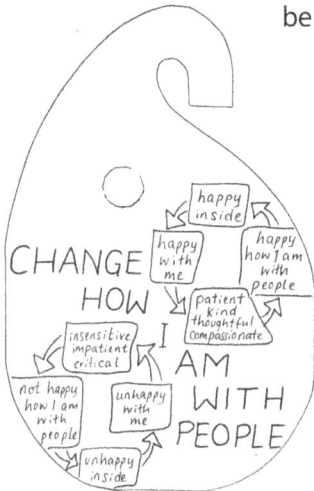

be less keeping me awake at night. There would be less for me to feel bad about. I would feel I was kind because I would be *being* kinder. I would feel I was gentle with people because I would be *being* gentle.

Okay, so of course I'm still not as wonderful as I would like to be, but by actively trying to be the person I want to be I'm a good bit nearer being a nice person, and I don't hate myself any more, in fact I quite like myself. And I am happy. I am grateful for that.

So apply this to writing.

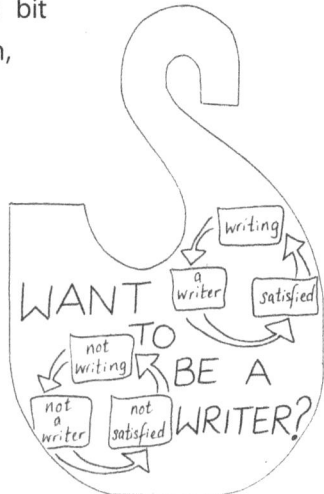

You want to be a writer? Then write. Be the person you want to be.

Being An Amateur – Doing It For Love (Not Money)

I have recently discovered that I do not like doing things for money.

It's not that I don't like money, I do like money, it's useful.

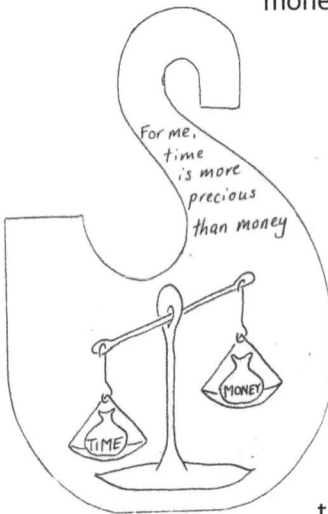

For me, time is more precious than money

MONEY

TIME

However, I am not particularly money-minded. Having money doesn't drive me in the way it drives some people. As long as I have enough to pay the bills, then once that is done, I'd much rather have time than money.

And it's not like I don't do things for money – of course I do. I go to work for money just like everyone else. I don't mind the job I do at the moment, but, let's face it, I wouldn't do it if I weren't getting paid.

The point I'm trying to make is that I have found that when I do something to get money for it, then I feel differently about it – I've found I feel different when I'm doing it, and I've found that what I produce is different.

So take my dressmaking, for example. I love making dresses. I make myself dresses almost all the time (when I'm not working, or writing, or drawing, or making other things). Several of my friends, and some people just in passing, have said to me that I could sell the dresses I make. This may or may not be true.

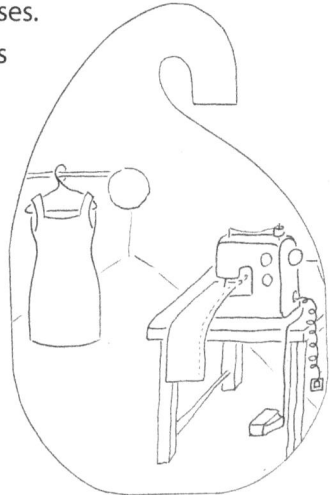

Near where I live, one or two villages away, is a craft centre where small stalls, workshops and boutiques are ranged round two floors of a converted farm building. On occasion I have found myself envying the women who spend their days at the back of their pretty little shops, making embroidered cards, patchwork children's play-tents, and lycra dancewear, presenting vintage clothing, and hand-made jewellery.

Earlier this year I texted my daughter after I had visited the craft centre and I asked her if she thought I could sell the dresses I make on such a stall: she thought I probably could.

I thought about it all morning. I mused on it while I swam my forty lengths of the pool in the leisure centre at the back of the local hotel. It didn't take me long to realise

I didn't want to make dresses in order to sell them.

It took me barely an hour or two of considering making ten dresses in the same style in different fabrics and different sizes for me to realise I would hate to do that.

BOREDOM OF REPETITION V. EXCITEMENT OF INVENTION

Each dress I make for myself is considered, thought about, designed, dreamt up. They are individuals that I have created. Dressmaking is something I love doing. It is something I choose to do, that's what makes it a passion rather than a job. If I spent all day making dresses I didn't want to make just in order to get money, it would stop being a passion and would turn into a job. I'd rather keep it as a passion. I want to carry on loving making dresses rather than sighing and wishing I didn't have to do it because I'd rather be making something else.

And then there's professionalism. If you're doing something for money, it makes you a professional. And if you're a professional, then there are certain rules about what you should do and people expect certain standards. That's a good thing. Totally. I'm not saying 'let's not have rules and standards'. But I am saying that when I'm making things I don't want to have to think too much about professionalism; I want to get things right for me; I want to do the best job I can do for me, whether it's a dress, or a drawing, or a piece of writing, or a small split-level wooden spice rack I'm designing for my kitchen wall.

This makes me an amateur – I love doing those things, I do them for love, not money. That's what being an amateur is all about: the word comes from the Latin word 'amare', to love.

One of the reasons I decided I didn't want to

become a professional counsellor, despite the urging of my tutors, was because I didn't want to do counselling for money – if I was going to offer people empathic and non-judgemental listening, I decided, I wanted to do it because I cared about them, not because they paid me.

Just because in some pursuits I don't want to be a professional, doesn't make professionalism a bad thing. It's important there are professional standards in so many fields, including counselling. I just didn't want to be involved in that. It's a choice thing.

Thankfully there are plenty of competent makers (and doers) who are happy to make (and do) things for money: they are the professional tailors and dressmakers, carpenters and joiners, professional artists and writers, designers and musicians,

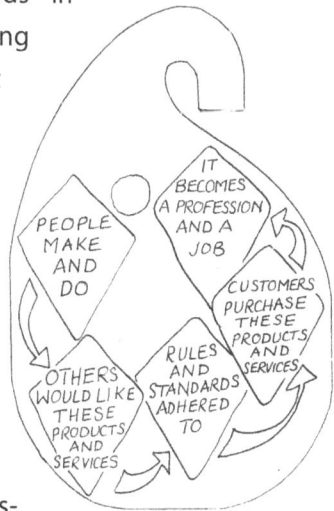

PEOPLE MAKE AND DO

IT BECOMES A PROFESSION AND A JOB

CUSTOMERS PURCHASE THESE PRODUCTS AND SERVICES

RULES AND STANDARDS ADHERED TO

OTHERS WOULD LIKE THESE PRODUCTS AND SERVICES

and counsellors, who produce things and provide services to a high standard and adhere to professional guidelines – if they didn't we wouldn't buy their products and services.

I'm happy to let them provide the professional products and services. I will quietly get on with doing the things I love doing, for the love of doing them.

And then there's choice...

"don't tell me what to do"

I feel differently about something when I feel I *have* to do it. I'm a stroppy person and I don't like being told what to do. I like to choose.

I feel even more strongly about something I *have* to do if I feel I have to do that thing in order to get money. If I *had* to do something for money, my heart just wouldn't be in it.

Once, a few years ago now, I briefly went out with a man who liked to gamble. He was very good at it. One of our first dates turned out to be a drive to a bookie's, where he put £20 on a greyhound for me, then came back from the counter with £100 that he insisted I put in my pocket.

We had a weekend away, including several expensive meals out; when we came home on the Sunday afternoon, this guy flicked on the tv and quietly cheered as he checked the results to find that the majority of his dogs and horses had come in as planned and his winnings covered the costs of our weekend away. Going to the races with him was a good deal of fun because he betted

so well. He knew a lot about horses, and greyhounds. [**Please note**: everyone else I've known who has been a gambler has lost money. It is a mug's game. This guy was the exception. Please don't think I am recommending gambling, I would urge you not to gamble anything you can't afford to lose. And, remember, gambling can also become addictive.]

During a conversation with this man when I was seeing him, my friends and I asked him why he carried on working when he won so much money by gambling. He then revealed that he had, in fact, been a professional gambler for a few years some ten years previously – he had approached it in a business-like manner, setting aside enough money for bills and expenses every month, and gambling only with the profits he had made the previous month. I was astonished, impressed. Prior to this, I had honestly believed no gambler could consistently come out on top, but this man proved me wrong – his expert knowledge about the form and bloodlines of greyhounds and horses meant he was more likely to win than not.

So, we asked him, why did you stop? If you were coming out on top, week on week, month on month, why did you stop gambling as a profession? His reply went something like this: by making it his profession, all the joy had gone out of it, he didn't enjoy gambling any more, it wasn't fun. He wasn't *choosing to do it*, for the excitement; he *had to do it* to pay the bills. That was the difference. And that's why he stopped. His heart wasn't in it any more. Gambling was such a source of pleasure for him that he wanted to return it to its original position: pursuit, pastime, project. Lucrative? Yes. Profession? No.

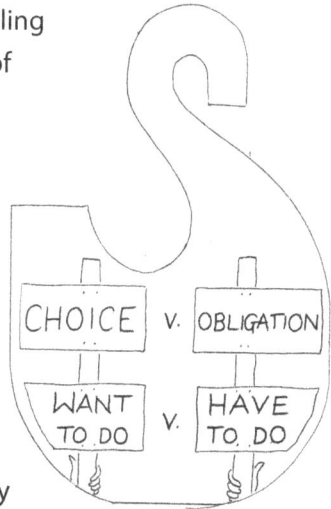

CHOICE v. OBLIGATION

WANT TO DO v. HAVE TO DO

Now I'd be delighted if it turned out, completely by coincidence, that someone out there was prepared to give me a large sum of money for something I'd made or written. If my chosen projects turned out to be as lucrative as gambling was for that former boyfriend of mine, I would welcome it. The thought tickles me pink. Inadvertent riches, what fun, like a fairy tale. I think it is highly unlikely this will happen however, so I have no plans to give up the day job just yet.[1]

I want to do the making, the drawing, the dressmaking, the writing just because I love doing those things – not for money, not because I have to, not because someone has placed an order, sent me a commission.

I want to do the making pure, neat, undiluted.

Any financial gain will be purely coincidental.

Do What You Love, And Love What You Do

So this phrase is a bit of a cliché: do what you love and love what you do. Perhaps it is

---

1   In one of his recent columns in the Guardian, Oliver Burkeman came to the same conclusion – for his thoughts, see After Words at the end of this book.

almost too catchy for its own good. Perhaps too many people have already said it.

That doesn't stop me wanting to say it again though.

I think it's important to keep saying things, even if there are not many people listening.

When I was delivering offending behaviour programmes to prisoners (which was a bit like running workshops and debates every morning for groups of ten troubled men who didn't really want to be there), one of the aims was to encourage the group members to alter their patterns of thinking – we hoped they would think of alternative, non-criminal ways out of sticky, tricky or pressurising situations in the future. We were optimists, those of us who worked in Programmes: we believed people could change, but we had also seen enough real life and prison life to know that people don't change overnight,

and that people only change when they really badly want to.

My colleagues in the Psychology Department of the prison showed me statistics from Canada where the R&R (Reasoning and Rehabilitation) Programmes had originated, and much of the research proved that thinking skills programmes did have some effect on some of the course participants. I can't remember the statistics now, and it's possible that there have been other surveys since that show different results.

I do believe people can change – I am my own evidence for this every day. I also believe that what we say to people can, sometimes, hit home. This is, I suppose, one of the reasons I write.

Often I think people are affected by what they experience and what they see, rather than what they are told – I'm pretty certain we are convinced by example, by being shown, more than by a lecture.

However, just occasionally, what we are told is delivered by the right person at the right time and in the right way – then it hits home.

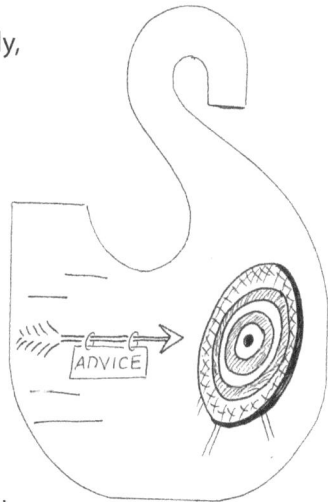

When I was delivering those Thinking Skills sessions to inmates in prison I had a rule of thumb, something to keep me going when I became demotivated:

It might be that only one person on each group heard and understood the point of an exercise. It might be that only one in ten people who understood then went on to change their thinking and behaviour because of what they heard. Nevertheless, one day in a few years' time, one of those prisoners from the group might just change what he was about to do because of something we said – we would never know, but if he was leading a slightly better life because of it, then it would have been worth it.

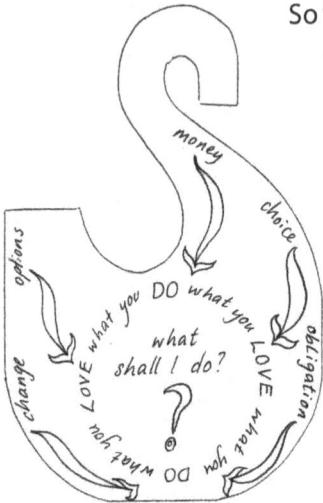

AHA!

STOP AND THINK!

So 'do what you love and love what you do' is a bit of a cliché, but it's still worth a mention. If only 1% of the people who read this book, take that phrase away and act on it, it is still worth saying it.

money

choice

options

obligation

change

LOVE what you DO what you LOVE what you DO what you

what shall I do?

THE SIX-DAY

'Do what you love and love v
came to me from my youngest
parked in a car park at a servi
one evening in the winter, on the ...
from rugby training. I was going through a
period of stress and depression; I had decided
I didn't want to become a counsellor, I was
finding the process of stopping and changing
difficult – if I didn't want to be a counsellor,
then what did I want to do with my life?
Inside me I was panicking: my children were
growing up, they were leaving home; some
message inside my head was telling me I had
to have my future mapped out before they
all left, I had to know what I wanted to be
before I was on my own otherwise…
otherwise…otherwise I felt I'd
fall into some kind of abyss.

My wise son, with all
the natural wisdom
and confidence of a
sixteen-year-old, said,
as he ate his fried
chicken, "Mum, you've
got to do what you love
and love what you do".

"Do what you love.
Love what you do."

Thinking of how far he had gone, and how much he had achieved by applying this principle, I could see how right he was. I realised I wasn't doing the things I loved with my life: I was working to earn a living, I was training in a field I used to love but had changed my mind about, I spent my spare time keeping house. Since then I have tried my hardest to do what I love. I stopped training to be a counsellor. I started making more clothes. I stopped doing what other people thought was a good thing. I started drawing and painting, and making things, and writing stories. Now I love what I do.

The phrase hit home. The right person said the right thing to me at the right time.

Only recently, two years later, did I discover where my son had got that phrase from.

I was standing next to my son's former rugby coach. He had coached my son at club level, now his son and mine played in the same U19s academy side. We were talking with the other parents, saying how much more confidence the team had this week compared to the week before – they were playing Leeds; they were still losing, but they were playing well and fighting until the end. We discussed the importance of psychology in sport, how the lads had to love what they were doing out there on the pitch. I mentioned what my son had told me in that dark car park when I was so depressed.

"Ha!" said my son's old coach, "I used to tell him that. That's what I used to tell the lads in training."

"Well, it paid off, didn't it? At least one of them was listening to you." I smiled as I replied. Not only had my son taken it to heart, but when he had told me, I had taken it to heart too. It had created a trickle down effect.

The right person had told my son in the right way at the right time, then my son passed the message on to me. The right person saying the right thing in the right way at the right time. Serendipity.

THE RIGHT PERSON
SAYING
THE RIGHT THING
IN THE RIGHT WAY
AT THE RIGHT TIME
IS
SERENDIPITY

Love versus money...choice versus duty...

Doing what you love and loving what you do is simple when it comes to us choosing what to do in our spare time, it seems to me. It becomes complicated if we try to involve 'loving what we do' into our day jobs, into our paid employment, into the things we do to earn a living. Here, I find, it is not always possible for 'love' to be involved.

As I discovered when I considered amateurism versus professionalism, I don't seem able to make myself love the things I do to make money.

If I set out to make money out of doing something, then I find I don't love that thing in the same way any more. When I thought about earning a living being a counsellor, I didn't want to do that any more; when I thought about making money out of dressmaking, I didn't want to do that either. The choice and the freedom had been taken out of it. For me it appears, I need to keep what I love doing separate from earning a living; some people in some professions are able to merge the two, but I'm not. I aim to have a job I don't mind doing, but I don't expect to love it. I keep 'love' for the things I am free to choose to do.

This may be because I'm stroppy and don't like being told what to do.

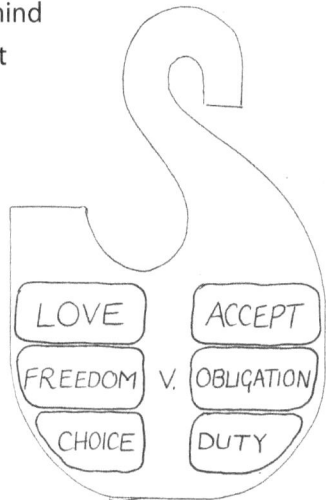

LOVE   ACCEPT

FREEDOM V. OBLIGATION

CHOICE   DUTY

As regards writing, it is of course possible to sit down and write with the intention of making money out of your writing. Journalists do this every day, ghost writers write books for others, you may hit on a very marketable idea for a book, and there are professional writers who are commissioned to write books for publishing houses on specific topics or themes.

Those jobs wouldn't suit me however, because the elements of freedom and choice would have been removed. It is as if I am only able to love doing something if I have freely chosen to do it. When it comes to making things – art, craft and writing – I don't like being told what to do, I guess.

Mapping What Works

I am visual. I like maps, drawings, plans and diagrams. Seeing things mapped out in front of me helps me understand. Ideas laid out in order, images arranged in a design, weaving a fabric of ideas, that's the sort of thing that works for me – it helps me untangle and sift through the jumble in my head, it helps me make sense of where I'm going – with my day, my week, a task, a project, a journey or a book.

You may have gathered how visual I am from the amount of illustrations in this book. I feel strongly that books for adults can and should be illustrated. Despite the fact that I read (and write) a good deal, my heart still sinks when I open a large book and there is nothing but text there. By contrast, my heart leaps with joy when there are illustrations, maps, diagrams, family trees, casts of characters,

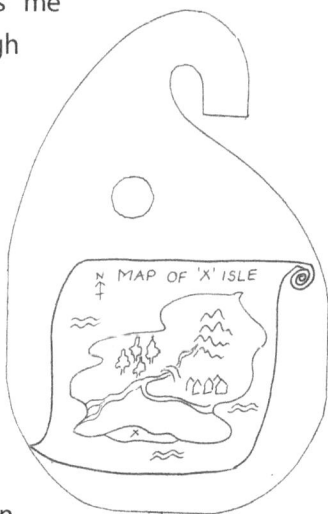

letters in different fonts; it brings the text to life for me.

You may also have noticed the good-sized margins in this book. I hope you have been having fun with these, writing in them, doodling, making your own notes if you want.

Every writer is as individual as the book they end up writing, so you will find what works for you. It may be worth jotting down what works for you and what doesn't, so you know how to work best to your strengths and which techniques to use again.

In the non-fiction books I read (and occasionally in fiction books, too) I keep a pencil to hand and I write notes in the margin. I can't stop myself. Things spring to mind while I am reading and I want to make a note of them, I want to tie in my thoughts with the ideas on the page. I want to jot down the examples from my life that illustrate the points the author is making. I want to underline the points I want to remember.

When I first noticed how much I wrote in books as I read them, I would tell myself that one day I would write a book from all the notes I made during my reading. But this is unlikely, since I probably don't have time to go back through all the books I've ever read and collect all the notes from the margins.

I think, in fact, I do this note-making process as a way of embedding the ideas I get from a book. I think it may be the process of making a mark on the paper that helps embed the idea or the understanding for me – almost as if the idea is the seed and the process of making a mark (writing it down, underlining or circling it, making notes or illustrations) is what plants the seeds and helps it germinate. That would explain why I take so many notes when I am studying.

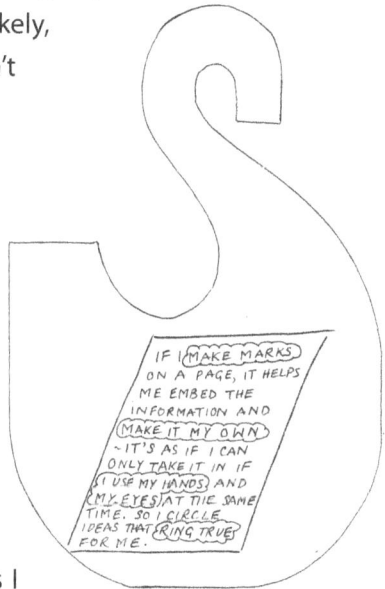

IF I MAKE MARKS ON A PAGE, IT HELPS ME EMBED THE INFORMATION AND MAKE IT MY OWN – IT'S AS IF I CAN ONLY TAKE IT IN IF I USE MY HANDS AND MY EYES AT THE SAME TIME. SO I CIRCLE IDEAS THAT RING TRUE FOR ME.

The process of writing things down shifts the ownership of the thought...from the author to me. The activity makes it part of me. A bit like how we need to try blowing on a trumpet to realise just how to make a sound from it. It is the doing process that makes the thing ours.

PLANTING A SEED

So use this book the way that works for you. Draw maps and diagrams, add your own doodles, jot notes in the margins and the boxes, highlight passages, circle words, add your own examples, make it yours.

If you plan to write your own book or are already doing so, then make sure you keep notes: notes are fuel to the fire; inspiration is the spark, but notes are fuel. The fire will soon fade if it doesn't have fuel.

Of course, you and I may find that what worked for us one time may not work for us next time we sit down to write a book, so then it's time to revise and review.

This brings me neatly on to the SE3R.

The SE3R Storyboard

When I first started writing this book earlier this year, a friend of mine, who is a police officer, called round for coffee one afternoon. I asked her about the interviewing course she had been on the previous week, and she mentioned a technique they had been taught called the SE3R.

SE3R stands for Survey, Extract, Read, Review, and Respond. It is an investigation tool devised by Dr Eric Shepherd.[2] The SE3R is used by police officers and other investigators to

2   See   http://www.forensicsolutions.co.uk/SE3R.htm   for further details.

gather and assess all the details from verbal statements by witnesses and others.

My friend explained how they had been taught to draft SE3R storyboards to record all the details from an interview, chronologically and in depth. As soon as my friend described the SE3R storyboard to me, I knew it was something that would appeal to me…I could visualise how it could be used to capture the events before, after and around an incident. I asked my friend to draw it for me. She drew something like this:

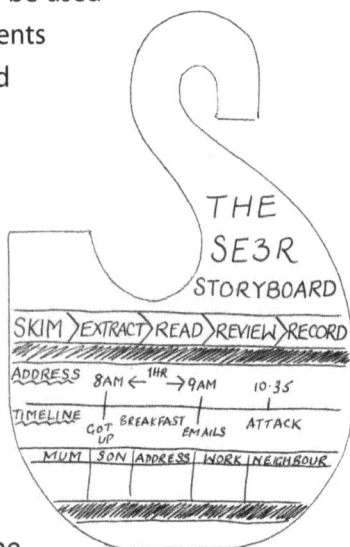

My friend was quick to point out that not every officer had taken to the SE3R storyboard with the enthusiasm she had; it worked for her, but it wouldn't work for everyone.

Storyboards work for some people; mood boards work for some people; lists, maps and plans work for some people and not others. We are the experts on ourselves – we can get to know ourselves and how best we work; we can try out different techniques, adapting and refining the ones we like, building our own toolkit of writing resources, keeping a folder, a portfolio, a physical (or metaphorical) shoebox of ideas.

And from time to time, we can review them – we may have changed.

SPIDER DIAGRAM

MIND MAP

BULLET LIST
• GUNS
• AMMUNITION
• POLICE
• THIEVES
• SCARING
• STREETS
• CLASH

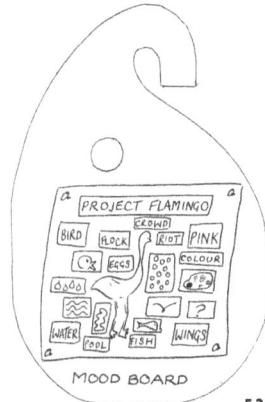

PROJECT FLAMINGO

MOOD BOARD

Completion – a Perfectionist in Recovery

Much of my life (it feels to me) I have spent not finishing things. That is perhaps the way of things – life does not always come in neatly finished off packages. Many things don't really finish, sometimes they just tail off, or they are torn apart, or we think they're finished and they crop up again. Or sometimes I find I don't get the chance to finish things the way I want. Or I change my mind.

Perhaps there just aren't neat endings in real life.

That stands to reason.

Daily life is not the same as a story – life goes on, stories come to an end.

Nevertheless, leaving things unfinished did (does) appear to be a bit of a habit of mine.

Among other things, my life boasts:

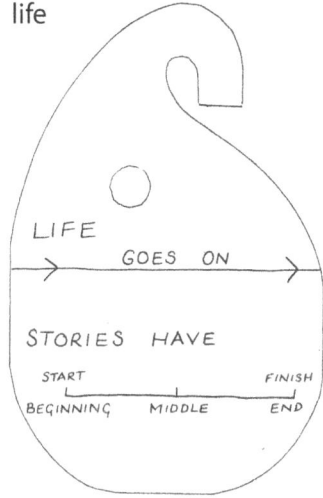

- unfinished projects (making a set of curtains for the summerhouse, for example)

- unfinished writing (half a dozen first chapters of novels, for example)

- unfinished courses (I didn't finish Psychology A level, and I only completed the first year of the Person-Centred Counselling degree)

- unfinished sewing (I have a chest of drawers of fabric, patterns, and half-made dresses)

and those are just the ones that immediately spring to mind.

I live with this trait (of not finishing things) happily much of the time.

Occasionally it gets to me.

That's when I need to finish something to prove to myself it can be done.

A friend of mine once told me I was not a 'completer-finisher'. I have since found out that a 'completer-finisher' is a name of a role within a work team, and the phrase (along with other descriptions of roles within teams) is used by managers in a business context.[3]

---

3   For team role descriptions, see: http://www.belbin.com/content/page/49/BELBIN(uk)-2011-TeamRole SummaryDescriptions.pdf).

At the time when my friend labelled me as 'not a completer-finisher' however, I just thought he meant I was someone who didn't finish things. I have a feeling it was around the time that I had given up on another false start to a novel – I had written the first three chapters. I'm not sure he knew about all the other things I had started and hadn't finished – but I did. They were on one of the back shelves of the metaphorical shed in my head. The phrase 'not a completer-finisher' stuck with me.

I had something to prove.

Not a completer-finisher, you say? Well, I'll show you.

Not perfect…but changing…

What I find interesting is that (now that I've done a little research into it), I see that the role of completer-finisher describes someone I used to be.

*"**Team Role**: Completer-Finisher

Contribution: Painstaking, conscientious, anxious. Searches out errors. Polishes and perfects.

Allowable Weakness: Inclined to worry unduly. Reluctant to delegate."

This sounds like the person I was forty, thirty, even fifteen or twenty years ago, but not now. What happened in between?

I used to be a perfectionist. I used to 'get things right' – according to the manual, the examinations board, the guide, according to the teachers and the experts. I used to be a good student. I

used to be an efficient and accurate proof-
reader and copy-editor.

I can still muster up some of those traits
now, if I need to. I can still follow a manual
accurately, and correct a manuscript with
attention to detail, if I have to do it for work.
But it's not natural to me now,
and it's not how I choose to
be if given a choice.

I'll tell you what
happened in between
then and now – I
relaxed.

STRESSED   RELAXED

V.

HAVE TO
GET
THINGS
RIGHT

it'll
be okay

Perfectionism was what
I diagnosed myself with in
those days: I thought there
was a 'right' and I wanted to get things
'right'.

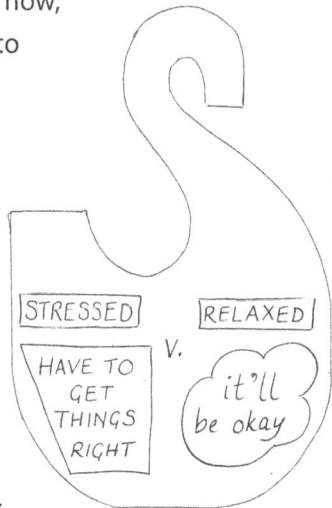

From the perspective of where I am now,
what I had looks like a mini obsession. I was

much more rigid about things than I am now. There was a wrong and a right, there was making 'a good job' of something and there was making 'a bad job' of something, and in the old days I used to put a fair bit of pressure on myself to make 'a good job' of almost everything I did.

So what happened?

In between then and now I have learnt to fail (a useful skill) and I have lived with my children (the best learning experience in the world).

And I suppose I had a few personal rock bottoms.

For a time, before I was forty, perfectionism was my addiction. And, as with many addictions, stress makes it worse and learning to relax makes things at least somewhat better.

I suppose I will always have some perfectionist traits, but now I am a perfectionist in recovery. Recovering addicts will understand.

At Perfectionists Anonymous I might say: "Hi. I'm Sass. I'm a perfectionist. But just for today I'm trying not to put pressure on myself to 'get things right'."

If that means I don't always finish things, that's okay. I'd rather be happy and relaxed among a pile of unfinished projects, than stressed and unhappy with everything complete.

Using anger to spur me on...

So the phrase my friend had used to describe me lodged in the part of my mind that used to be a perfectionist, and it grated and irritated like a grain of sand in an oyster.

'Sass, you're just not a completer-finisher.' My friend probably used that phrase to me

in 2006. Years later, it was still grating and irritating. I still felt as if I had something to prove. I still hadn't finished any of the novels I'd started.

And that's where this story started…

PART TWO – MAKING AND DOING (WHAT ACTUALLY HAPPENED)

The Build-Up

A few years ago (it was 2010, I remember, because it was a World Cup year, the vuvuzela one) my mum and I went away for a long weekend to stay in a house that belonged to some friends of hers.

2010 WORLD CUP

It was a super house, spacious but snug at the same time: there were comfortable through-rooms downstairs and cosy cottage bedrooms upstairs. It was tucked into an un-made-up track, off a road outside Marlowe. The house had a lovely garden: small French windows from the side of the living room opened on to a couple of steps down to a stone terrace and a big lawn stretched down to a little stream. It was July. The sun shone.

For some reason, we had decided this was going to be a writing weekend. I seem to remember I wanted to write a short story. Perhaps I just wanted to write something that I actually finished.

My mum and I get on. We really get on. She is my mum, I love her because of that, but also I think the world of her. I am constantly impressed by her – she is one of the nicest people

I know; she loves to please people and is genuinely kind in a way that I so often fail to be; she remembers to think about other people and says 'yes' when I would say 'no'. She is fabulously creative (she hates that word, so I thought I'd use it about her just to annoy her). The list of creative things my mum has done in her life is really long, so I'm not going to put it in here – in fact, I'll write another book about it one day, so you can find out then.

It is enough to say here that my mum (in her seventies) still draws, paints, and writes, and she runs a couple of creative writing workshops a month. Over the years, I have been to some (seriously, only two or three maximum) of my mum's writing workshops – with mixed results. I have always been overwhelmed by how good my mum is at her job: she is confident and assertive and motivational; she sets great exercises; she gives positive and helpful feedback, even while being honest. However, I haven't always felt very good about my own writing.

I didn't think of myself as a writer. I always felt I was a bit of an interloper in writing groups – I could put the pen on the paper but I couldn't make it write interesting words. Where was my imagination? Did I even have one? Where was the fourteen-year-old girl who loved English composition exams better than anything else? Was it writing emails and reports at work that had squashed all the creativity and inventiveness out of me? What had years of perfectionism done to the messy artsy person I used to be?

So perhaps I was challenging myself, that summer weekend in 2010. Perhaps I was willing myself to be a little different, to loosen up. Like a shy and awkward person finally flinging themselves on to the dancefloor. Perhaps that was what I was after, perhaps I wanted a safe space to explore letting go.

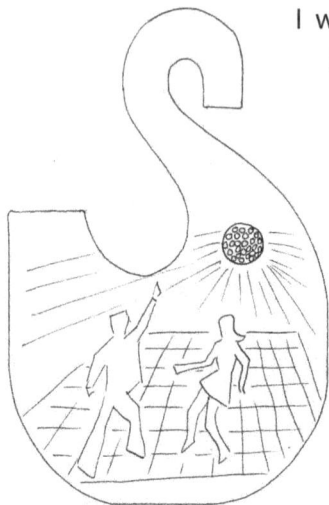

For me, there is nowhere safer than a cosy cottage with my family. I hope you have some people in your life with whom you can *really* be yourself, warts and all, crazy dancing, bizarre ideas. I hope you have somewhere safe where you can relax and let go. (In a safe and healthy way, of course.)

Virginia Woolf said, to be a writer, a woman needs 'a room of one's own'.[4]

And what I say is that you don't need that room of your own *all the time*. Unless you want to write every single moment of the day, you only need that space from time to time.

_____

4   *A Room of One's Own,* by Virginia Woolf. 1945, Penguin, London.

When mum and I went away for that first writing weekend of ours, we were making ourselves 'a room of our own' for the weekend. We were chiselling out a safe space where I could try my hand at writing a short story, and where she would get round to writing her book about doodling that she had an idea for.

So let's think about the ingredients in the mix.

We're already beginning to get a picture of the things that I needed in place in order to write.

Faith and love, I've already mentioned them in the previous section.

We could also call them belief and willingness.

Or confidence (in my ability) and desire.

Or possibility and inclination.

Or 'I can' and 'I want'.

I needed to believe I could write a bit, at least string a sentence together or describe a situation to a friend. And I needed to want to write *for its own sake*, for the love of doing it.

In a way, nothing ever gets off the ground if we don't

a) Believe it is possible and

b) On some level, want to do it.

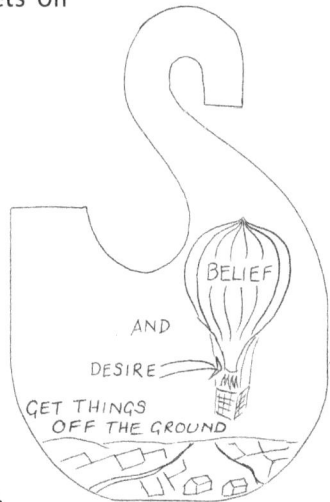

BELIEF

AND

DESIRE

GET THINGS
OFF THE GROUND

Those are the foundations.

Then we're going to need some practical things in place as well in order to be able to make this writing thing happen

From that first writing weekend away with my mum, now that I look back, I can see that it taught me that I also needed space and a like-minded supporter. So let's add them to my list:

1. **FAITH –** Belief in my ability

2. **LOVE –** Wanting to have a go

3. **SPACE –** Safe space to relax and be inventive (and to get things wrong)

4. **SUPPORT –** Someone who understands me and gives me the right kind of support

You, of course, may be different to me. You may be able to soldier on with just a shred of belief in yourself and overwhelming desire to achieve your goal. You may be able to write your book in cramped chaotic surroundings, and with no one cheering you on or giving you useful feedback. Cool. Good for you. If you can do that, I am immensely impressed and I take my hat off to you. I doubt whether I could. Maybe now that I know I can finish something, maybe now I know I can actually write 60,000 words with a start, a middle and an end, maybe now I could keep going on a diet of faith and love alone. But I know I wouldn't have got off the ground if it hadn't been for mum and me cutting ourselves out a little slice of July sunshine for a few days during the first week of the World Cup 2010.

That weekend I did write a short story, and I seem to remember I also tried writing a second one that wasn't quite so good. And I wrote a job application. I didn't get the job.

Mum started writing her doodle book and painted some pictures (she's more of an artist than a writer these days), and in the evening she would read what I'd written and we discussed the bits I wasn't sure about, what I could do to improve them. That was usually after we'd watched some of the football and eaten supper together.

The next time we went away together on our own, mum and me, was in the autumn of 2012. For my birthday, I asked mum if she would come away to a cottage for another writing weekend. Only this time it was mid-week. And we picked a cottage from a website. And we went to Derbyshire not the Welsh border.

But apart from that, I wanted to re-create the atmosphere we'd achieved two years previously; I wanted to try my hand at writing again. And I wanted the company and feedback mum provides. In fact, often she doesn't really need to say very much in the way of criticism and feedback because it is mainly the fact that I am *sharing* what I've written that is important – because I write differently when I know someone's going to read it, it becomes less like notes or a diary and more like a publication, it gains weight somehow.

I'm going to add that ingredient to the list – sharing. So now the list looks like this:

WRITING TO BE HEARD

1. **FAITH** – Belief in my ability

2. **LOVE** – Wanting to have a go

3. **SPACE** – Safe space to relax and be inventive

4. **SUPPORT** – Someone who understands and gives the right kind of support

5. **SHARING** – An audience, whether they give feedback or not

One of the other things about both our first two writing breaks was that there was no signal, no wifi. There was television, we took books and paints, there were local shops and pubs, so it wasn't as if there were no distractions at all. But, importantly for me, we were detached from our usual lives, our friends and family couldn't reach us, just for those few days. I think that goes into the 'space' category.

During our 2012 writing week (four days) I started writing something a bit longer than a short story, mainly because I'd had ideas for a setting, a character or two, some events which would go on for longer than a short story does. I'd had two or three ideas actually, and they kept getting knotted up in my head. The first evening we arrived I wanted to unravel them and make them into a coherent story that I could start writing the next day. I can remember mum suggesting they sounded like two stories, but I still wanted to weave them into one. I wrote pretty much for four days solidly, with breaks for freezing walks round the village (it was an icy November week), a visit to the local church (the 'cathedral of the peaks'), delicious pastries from the nearest shop, and supper and reading sessions with mum. I wrote three or four chapters, of varying quality and coherence, which got a few of my ideas out but tailed off into nothing. I had thought I knew where I was going, but I didn't. I still think there were probably at

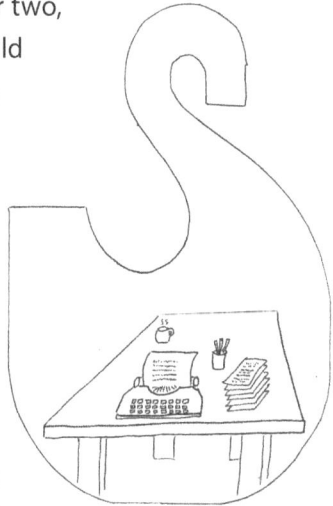

least two if not three concepts for stories there. Mum was right.

What I hadn't done was map out where I was going after the first few scenes.

I just didn't know the story, no wonder I couldn't tell it.

Third Time Lucky

I've always felt lucky.

It's a blessing.

I don't mean it's a blessing to be lucky, I mean it's a blessing to *feel* lucky.

I think I have also been fortunate: fortunate as regards the experience life has thrown at me as well as fortunate in the temperament

I have been given. I believe luck is 'made' as well as stumbled upon – I had a good start (thanks mum and dad), I made some decisions that were right for me (thanks me), some things went my way (thanks kids) and some didn't, and that's life.

What I mean about *feeling lucky* is probably something to do with optimism.

BORN CHEERFUL

I have rose-tinted glasses most definitely, and when I look back at some of my past it looks great and I have to remind myself of the reality of some of it (because it wasn't all great at the time). And I'm pragmatic also. So when something I don't like happens, then I rationalise it to myself as a 'useful learning experience'. This trait irritates my children, you may imagine. There's nothing more annoying than someone (like me) who tries to encourage you to see what you can learn from a really bad day when all you want is a big hug and a shoulder to cry on.

These optimistic traits I may have picked up from my mum. An illustration of how my mum can twist circumstances to see the silver lining comes from nearly 30 years ago. I was living in France for a year as part of my degree, working as an English Assistant teaching English conversation in two schools. My mum and dad had come over for a visit for a few days and they had brought my boyfriend with them. It was a Monday. It was raining. It was lunchtime, we were hungry, but unfortunately many places to eat were closed on a Monday in the little town in Burgundy in which I lived at the time. And we were running late, as usual. My dad (always a bit of a curmudgeon) was getting crosser and crosser. My boyfriend and I sat in the back of the car keeping quiet, all our suggestions for places to eat had fallen flat. As the rain fell dismally, and we circled the little town looking for anywhere that would sell us an omelette or a croque-monsieur, my mum came out with: "Isn't France beautiful in the rain!" This phrase has gone down in family history, you can imagine. If anyone can find a bright side to a miserable situation, it'll be my mum.

Or me.

Despite irritating people sometimes, I think feeling lucky is a blessing and it has enabled me to love my life – not every single moment of course, but generally speaking.

So I do believe in luck – the made kind and the given kind. I believe it because I feel it.

Mum and I had enjoyed our two previous writing trips, I wanted to repeat that but on a grander scale. This time was going to be third time lucky.

The Countdown and The Word Count

Our third writing trip away was going to be different from the others, in one major way. It was going to be longer. I asked mum if she would go away with me for a week. For me to write all week. To be frank, she didn't take that much persuading. And anyway, it was going to be the week before my 50th birthday, how could she refuse? It was my birthday treat after all.

Right from the start of 2013 we were planning to have a writing week away in November.

It was only by the spring I think that I was thinking about attempting to write a whole story in that week however.

A conversation about something else completely got me thinking about just how many words there are in a book.

I went upstairs and got a small novel from the shelves (I didn't need to get a big novel – I was never intending to write a family saga spanning four generations and a century).

I actually counted how many words there were on several randomly-selected pages, then multiplied it by the number of pages in the book. From this, I decided that 60,000 words was a minimum acceptably novel-sized book. Of course, slim novels, novellas, etc. are smaller. And many books are bigger. But anything less than 60,000 words wouldn't really feel novel-sized to me, it wouldn't really feel like a proper book in my hands. Totally a personal thing. You shouldn't be put off writing something smaller (or bigger) just because of my arbitrary novel size definitions.

So I counted words and pages.

60,000 words.

1,000 words is a couple of sides of A4, right?

300 words x 200 pages
= 60,000 words
= 1 novel

60,000

When I had written things before (essays, reports) I always had to cut words. My life has been a one-woman endless struggle against the wordcount. Why do exams and essays ask you an interesting big question and then tell you to give your views in a measly couple of thousand words? Ridiculous, I say. I knew that writing sheer numbers of words would not be a problem for me. If I am any kind of a writer, I am a marathon runner not a sprinter.

60,000 words was certainly a marathon.

Longer than anything I'd ever written before, much longer. Probably about ten times longer.

60,000 words though…just 120 pages.

'Do you know what?' I said slowly to myself, after counting the words and doing the mental calculations, sitting cross-legged on the floor. 'That's actually do-able…'.

And there. My light-bulb moment.

No great dream of writing a novel.

No burning ambition.

No earth-shattering blockbuster idea that had to find expression in print.

Just the simple, sheer do-ability of 60,000 words.

From then on, the plan began to take hold.

Firstly, it definitely had to be a week away for writing this year. I felt certain that a week would give me a chance to get a 60,000-word book at least well underway.

We booked the cottage in the late spring. A Derbyshire village again, no signal (I hoped) and the week before my 50th birthday. We carefully chose a cottage in the centre of the village, so we could walk easily to shops, cafes, pubs if we wanted. Equally, we carefully chose a village that was not too exciting. I wanted somewhere we could walk round in half an hour, just for a breath of fresh air, and most definitely somewhere without so many tourist attractions that we would want to stop what we were doing to go visit them.

As it happened, against all my careful plans, the craft centre at the old hall at the other end of the village had a ceramic painting workshop, which was open on Thursday and Friday. I love painting ceramics and seeing the colours come to life vividly when they are fired so I promised myself I would allow myself an afternoon off at the end of the week if I had written enough.

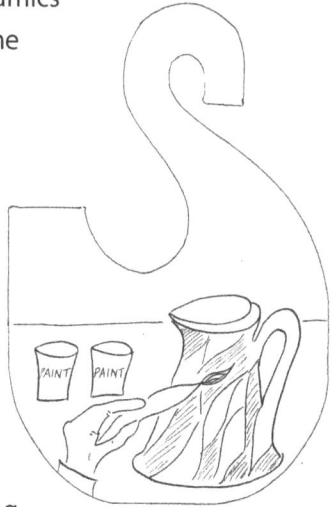

By the end of the week I was so close to finishing the book, I couldn't afford to take the afternoon off. I didn't feel sad though – I had a different kind of pleasure almost tangibly within my grasp.

Beginning to Plot

Over the summer I began to work out my plan. I don't think I told anyone but mum and the kids about it at this stage. Too many people knowing my ideas too early on can put me off them. A select few in on the act works better for me. I don't share very well.

I knew my autumn was going to be busy – we had a holiday to Crete booked in September, and October was going to be taken up with making Christmas presents – and, of course, work, earning a living, paying the bills and running the house had to happen alongside any creative plans I had.

This left me the summer to get some ideas down on paper.

The year before (during our writing trip) I had read the first few pages of *The Craft of Novel-Writing* by Dianne Doubtfire, and flicked through a section on devising a plot.

She advised dividing a novel into 30 sections and knowing what happened in each of those sections.[5]

I really loved the '30 sections' idea. Thirty sections fit so neatly on one side of ruled A4.

You can write the numbers down the left-hand side and then jot down ideas on the right.

Or you can make yourself a table or spreadsheet on your computer that looks like this one on the next page.

---

5   *The Craft of Novel-Writing,* by Dianne Doubtfire. 1987, Allison & Busby, London. P.11.

Scene no.	What happens in each section (scene)
1	
2	
3	
4	
5	
6	
7	
8	
9	
10	
11	
12	
13	
14	
15	
16	
17	
18	
19	
20	
21	
22	
23	
24	
25	
26	
27	
28	
29	
30	

And you can do it over and over again until you've got a plan that you like.

60,000 words divided by 30 sections = 2,000 words per section

Whenever I had an hour to spare, I'd have a little think and a little look at my plan. Mainly these moments happened in coffee shops, or in the car when I was waiting for my son – my youngest was a rugby league player (they play summer rugby) and I watched every match he played that season.

I knew I wanted to write an exciting story, something with action and suspense. I wanted to keep myself going as I wrote it, I knew I would need it to race along at a fair pace, I knew I would need *me* to be excited about what was going to happen next. So I wanted at least one

thing to happen in each section, possibly two things, so each thing (or event) would be written in 1,000 words. I reckoned that if I had one 'happening' every 2,000 words that might get a bit too slow and descriptive and I thought that if I had an event or a happening (an action, some movement or change) every 1,000 words, then this book would bounce along at a rollicking pace.

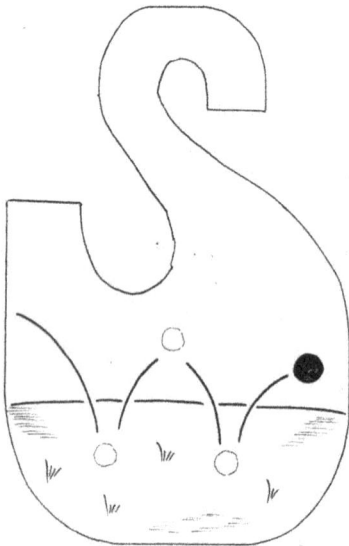

Now my page began to look a bit like this:

Section no.	Happening I	Happening II
1		
2		
3		
4		
5		
6		
7		
8		
9		
10		
11		
12		
13		
14		
15		
16		
17		
18		
19		
20		
21		
22		
23		
24		
25		
26		
27		
28		
29		
30		

Writing by Numbers

The first few scenes came to my mind pretty quickly one morning because I'd thought of my main character and I had a feeling I knew what this person was haunted by, driven by. I also had a picture in my mind of where (an actual location) I wanted my main character to end up about mid-way through the book. This was a bit random and was just because we were passing a place like this in the car one day.

I'll be honest, I'm not the most automatically imaginative person in the world. There are, possibly, people who can conjure up wonderful stories out of absolutely nothing. That's not me. I have to go looking for the ideas, I have to tease them out, I have to go digging and probing around in life and in my

DIGGING FOR TREASURE

own head, I have to go collecting stuff, and sometimes I have to give myself little jumping off grounds to get myself started. I suppose that's a bit like setting myself a little exercise to get me going.

Writing practice

My mum got me to write a poem from an exercise once, when we sat on a bench huddled in our fleeces looking out towards Dunstanburgh Castle on the Northumberland coast. My cousins' dogs were lying at our feet.

The exercise goes like this:

a.   Choose six words to describe the moment – don't think too long about it, pick them almost out of the air.

b.   Choose the one you least expected to turn up on your list.

c. Write three lines to describe the moment in terms of this word you have chosen.

d. Choose a word that brings uncertainty – 'if', 'maybe', or 'perhaps' – and fit it in at the start of the poem.

This is what I wrote:

KETTLE

If I am on and nearly boiling

Like the waves under Castle Rock

Like dog, I am a trusted friend

Like dog, you can call me black.

I was quite pleased with that. And I am not someone who is that big on poetry, I left that up to my mum. She was the poetry writer.

I think it's a good exercise so I wanted to include it in here. And I wanted to include it because it shows what can come out of a five-minute exercise.

I am not a poet. I don't write poetry, I don't read poetry, I skipped poetry options at school, I chose to read virtually no poets at university (apart from Dante, but reading Dante was obligatory and well worth the effort). I'm not that into poetry at all. I've made my point. But from a quick little exercise I had all the satisfaction of whipping out a little poem, fully formed. Great.

Don't dismiss exercises. If they can encourage me to write a poem, then, for me, they are almost miraculous.

Back to my point.

What I was saying was that I have an imagination (we all do) but I am more than aware that I need to cultivate and stimulate and encourage my imagination.

I took some of my favourite thrillers off the shelf and I studied their opening paragraphs. I looked at what happened in that first scene, I looked at how quickly it moved on to the next scene. I tried my hand at doing my own version of some of them, replacing their characters with my own, replacing their locations with my own, replacing their events with my own – I wasn't copying (I reasoned), I was simply using their first page structure as a template for practice.

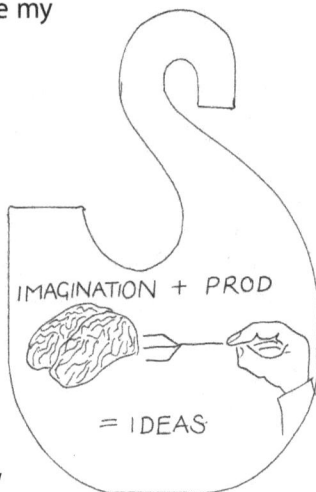

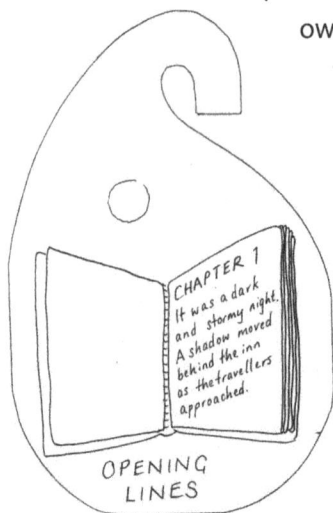

IMAGINATION + PROD

= IDEAS

CHAPTER 1
It was a dark
and stormy night.
A shadow moved
behind the inn
as the travellers
approached.

OPENING
LINES

If we like reading, and if we read a lot, I am sure

many aspects of stories and storywriting filter into our imaginations – turns of phrase, style, structure, devices – and they will come out in our own writing naturally. We don't need to *copy* old masters directly to learn to paint, but certainly looking at paintings will inform and inspire our own painting.

And we all have to get our ideas and influences from somewhere, right?

My first scene just sprung into my head soon after I'd spent my morning deep in the study of my favourite thriller first pages.

I decided I wanted plenty of strong female characters, because I am fed up with great stories being spoilt for me by being led by men all the time. My life is full of women. Yes, I have sons and a brother, and my friends have husbands, and I have male colleagues and male friends, but I know dozens of interesting and funny and exciting and characterful women. I wanted a book that felt more like my life than some movie where the only female role is the love-interest about two-thirds of the way through.

So I listed my characters and started working though my scenes – two events to a scene, each scene 2,000 words, roughly.

I called my characters A, B, C, D, etc. at this planning stage, because I was just jotting down notes and getting a shape to the twists and turns of the story. But that was a mistake. A, B, C and so on stuck, and I found myself calling them A and B through the story. Then it was hard to shake off.

A = Adam
B = Bethany
C = Conrad
D = Dionne

CHARACTER NAMES

You may find you don't have this problem. You may call your characters A, B and C, or 1, 2 and 3 and find it doesn't affect your relationship with them, cool. For me, however, I found I got stuck thinking of them by the letter and ended up having to name them after the letter I'd used in my notes, silly me. Won't do that again.

Perhaps this serves as a reminder to me to be careful how I refer to things in my notes, because I may find it difficult to change something I get used to in the planning stage.

This also indicates how important it is to do the work at this planning stage, because this is where I had to iron everything out; everything had to be set at planning stage because I knew there was going to be no time to re-plan anything when I was writing.

With six days to write 60,000 words, there would be no time to do anything but write.

A week or two before we went away, I realised I didn't actually know how long it would take me to write 60,000 words. There I was planning to write 60,000 words in a week and I didn't even know if it could be done.

Goodness, that could've scuppered my plans at the final hurdle.

I had been working on the assumption that 500 words was about a side of A4 and surely I could write two sides of A4 in an hour. But I didn't know for sure. So, with barely a fortnight before kick-off, I tested myself: I timed myself making up and writing two short passages of 1,000 words each. I could just about manage to write 1,000 words in an hour.

1,000 words = 1 hour

This was a relief – but it was also slightly worrying. I hadn't found it as easy as I'd hoped – imagining, inventing, describing, writing under time pressure was going to be no easy task. I would have no time to dawdle or daydream – in order to write 1,000 words in an hour I would have to do nothing but write.

Six Days

We arrived in the dark.

It's quite exciting to arrive at a holiday house in the dark I find, because I have two revelations: the first discovery is finding and exploring the house the first night, and then the second unveiling is the next morning when I see the surroundings in daylight.

We arrived in the dark because, despite the fact that the Derbyshire cottage was only an hour or two's drive from our house in Lancashire, I wanted to stay home to watch the rugby league world cup semi-final before we left. Mum, obliging as always, said she didn't mind – I was driving anyway, she had no choice.

ARRIVING
IN THE DARK

That first evening all we did was settle in.

We chose our rooms, and unpacked a little, although this wasn't easy because the cottage was so small there was only a very limited amount of wardrobe and drawer space. This didn't bother us much however, because we weren't on holiday and only needed a couple of sets of jeans and jumpers.

Then we walked across the square to the village shop in the dark, and bought bread, milk, kindling and a bag of logs for the wood burner. We had brought food with us for our first meal, so we made supper and lit the fire.

After supper, without giving away my ideas for the story, I explained to mum how I had planned the plot and what I hoped to do in the week ahead.

This is what my plan looked like:

> Day 1 – write 10,000 words
>
> Day 2 – write 10,000 words
>
> Day 3 – write 10,000 words
>
> Day 4 – write 10,000 words
>
> Day 5 – write 10,000 words
>
> Day 6 – write 10,000 words

Mum knew I wanted to finish the story in a week, she knew I'd be pressed for time, so she had brought her own projects with her and always had her drawing and painting things to hand.

I explained that I would write for ten hours, or until I had completed my 10,000 words, and then mum could read what I'd written that day while I made supper. That was the plan. I also explained to mum what sort of feedback I wanted. Mum's great at doing just what I ask her to, and she's a very devoted parent; she already loves everything I do so it wouldn't be difficult for her to be encouraging.

> *Feedback I wanted to hear:*
>
> ➤ "Well done for making the wordcount for the day!"
>
> ➤ "Keep going, you're doing well."
>
> ➤ "Remember it's all about getting it done."
>
> ➤ "You can always edit and revise later, this week is about completion."

When it came to the first evening, I made a second copy of the story saved under 'mum's version' and showed mum how to add comments on to a word document. In this way, if she did have queries or criticisms, she could comment on what I'd written but I didn't need to worry about it now – I could save her comments for later, when I was doing revisions. This would help me to keep the writing separate from the editing and revising function.

I knew myself well enough to know that if I got bogged down in wondering if my writing was any good, or if I started to go back and read over passages and make changes, then fiddling with the story like that would bring down the whole house of cards and I'd not get it finished in the week.

The only way I could get a 60,000-word story written in a week was to write and do nothing else.

To write and not read it back.

To write and not worry about whether it was any good.

My days would look like this, I planned:

7am   get up and have a cup of tea, turn the heating up and put some music on

7.30   start writing, write for an hour

8.30   have breakfast and get washed and dressed

9 am continue to write, write for two hours

11am   have a tea break and chat to mum, or walk up the village

11.30   write again, for another two hours

1.30   take a break for lunch; walk over to the little café across the square and try one of their delicious soups, possibly take a half-hour's stroll in the village

2.30   back to my writing desk, this time for three hours

5.30   tea break and chat to mum, maybe a slice of cake or a piece of fruit to keep going

6pm   back to writing again, the final two-hour session

8pm   finish for the day, make supper for mum while she reads the latest chapters

Writing out the plan like this, I can see what a hard task I had set myself. I tried to stick to the plan, but I didn't. The first day we took a long mid-morning break to explore the village; another afternoon we had a walk after lunch; one day mum even went over to the café on her own for lunch, because I had to keep going with the writing to catch up.

I was exhilarated by the whole project.

I knew I'd set myself a hard task, but I also knew it was technically achievable. I simply needed to put the plan into practice.

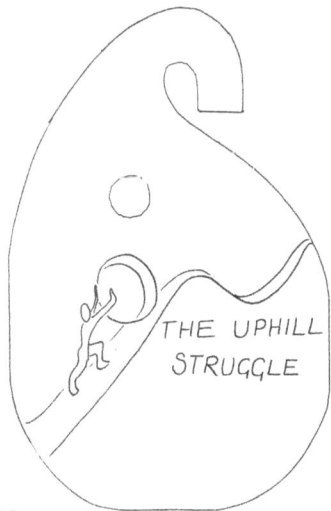

THE UPHILL STRUGGLE

The reality was, however, that for most of the first part of the week I was running slightly behind on the wordcount and by mid-week (Tuesday and Wednesday) I was feeling slightly down about it – it felt as if what I was writing was rubbish, and I wasn't even going to get it finished. Tuesday night was the evening I felt most miserable. I think this was mostly mid-term blues however, because by the Thursday, I was excited by what I was writing again and I could see the end in sight.

If you look at the statistics below,

Day	Words	Total
Sunday	9356	9356
Monday	9264	18620
Tuesday	8973	275593
Wednesday	14417	42010
Thursday	9577	51587
Friday	8916	60503

you can see that (apart from the final day when it was nearly finished anyway) I wrote the least number of words on the Tuesday – 8,973. That's 1,027 off my 10,000-word target for the day. If I'd carried on at that rate I would have fallen more than 4,000 words short of my 60,000-word novel. You can see why I was depressed, I feared I wouldn't achieve my goal. The following day – the Wednesday – I made a huge effort. This may have been the day I worked through lunch. I was desperate to get my wordcount up again. I hadn't set out to write a bestseller. I wasn't writing great literature. It wasn't even the novel I'd always dreamed of writing. I had only one goal, and that was to complete a story of at least 60,000 words by the end of the week. If I didn't manage that, I would have failed.

So spurred on by the low of Tuesday, and finally getting my main character into the place I wanted him by the middle of the novel, I wrote a whopping 14,417 words on the Wednesday. Finally I was ahead of my target of minimum 10,000 words per day.

Words

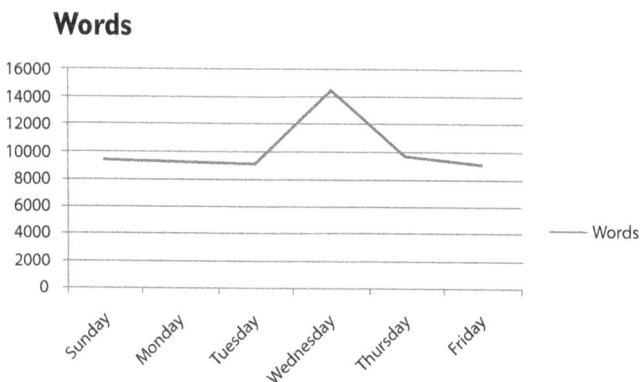

After this, it was much plainer sailing. I felt I knew where I was going, there was light at the end of the tunnel, the characters had eased into me, the story rolled along with a momentum of its own – despite some of my crazier flights of fancy.

As I completed my allotted number of words for the day on Thursday, I bounded in to mum and said: "Mum, do you know what?! I'm going to get it done. I'm really going to get this story finished!" And then, only then, did I realise that, when I finished it, I would have written a novel in a week and written a book before my 50th birthday.

Targets can be funny things. We need targets, we need deadlines, we need plans and timetables; we need these things sometimes to spur us on to achieve our goals. I would probably not have written that story if I hadn't set myself the challenge of writing a book in a week.

On the other hand, too much pressure can be stifling.[6] If I had told myself I had to write a novel before I was 50 years old, I probably would've backed out. The deadline would have squashed out my enthusiasm. It might have seemed too big a task.

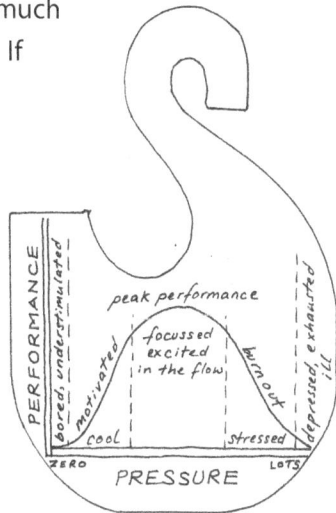

I knew full well that it was my 50th birthday on the Saturday. I had it all planned: my two eldest were coming up from uni for the weekend, mum and I were joining the children at Old Trafford to watch the rugby league world cup, then we were going to book into an apartment in the city for the weekend with my brother and his girlfriend, my children and my extra son (my youngest's best mate) and finally we would go out for a Thai meal in Manchester. So I definitely knew it was my birthday.

---

6   For more on the performance-arousal curve, see: https://en.wikipedia.org/wiki/Yerkes%E2%80%93Dodson_law.

And I definitely knew I planned to write a book in a week when mum and I went away to write.

I just hadn't tied the two together until the Thursday before I finished. It was only then that I realised that I would have written a novel before I was 50. It may seem bizarre, but I hadn't put two and two together. I can be dumb like this sometimes.

If I'd planned it, I honestly believe it wouldn't have happened. If I'd set myself the task of writing a novel before I was 50, it would have been too much pressure, too close a deadline, too big an achievement to aim for. I needed a challenge, but nothing too big.

The Statistics

Since this writing week was about getting numbers of words down on paper, I loved seeing the wordcount grow. It was like my very own telethon, watching the total grow each hour, each day. I loved to work out my words-per-hour rate during my tea breaks: Was I on target? Did I need to up the words-per-hour in order to achieve my total for the day?

Okay, this won't appeal to everyone. But it amuses me to think about figures. I do the same when I'm swimming lengths – I have my average number of lengths I do in five minutes, for example, and some days I'm interested to see that I've been doing more than my average and can take an extra couple of minutes in the Jacuzzi before getting on with my day.

SWIMMING P

40 lengths in 30 minutes

You can see how my figures for the week stacked up from the table on the next page.

Day	Date	Scene	Words	Total
Sunday	24/11/2013	1	2626	2615
Sunday	24/11/2013	2	1797	4412
Sunday	24/11/2013	3	3603	8015
Sunday	24/11/2013	4	1341	9356
Monday	25/11/2013	5	2859	12215
Monday	25/11/2013	6	1689	1689
Monday	25/11/2013	7	1545	15449
Monday	25/11/2013	8	2137	17586
Monday	25/11/2013	9	1034	18620
Tuesday	26/11/2013	10	2265	20885
Tuesday	26/11/2013	11	1937	22822
Tuesday	26/11/2013	12	2189	25011
Tuesday	26/11/2013	13	2582	27593
Wednesday	27/11/2013	14	2945	30538
Wednesday	27/11/2013	15	1067	31605
Wednesday	27/11/2013	16	1851	33456
Wednesday	27/11/2013	17	1042	34498
Wednesday	27/11/2013	18	1724	36222
Wednesday	27/11/2013	19	954	37176
Thursday	28/11/2013	20	4834	42010
Thursday	28/11/2013	21	1625	43635
Thursday	28/11/2013	22	428	44063
Thursday	28/11/2013	23	1706	45769
Thursday	28/11/2013	24	2505	48274
Thursday	28/11/2013	25	810	49084
Thursday	28/11/2013	26	1607	50691
Friday	29/11/2013	27	896	51587
Friday	29/11/2013	28	647	52234
Friday	29/11/2013	29	2314	54548
Friday	29/11/2013	30	793	55341
Friday	29/11/2013	31	1776	57117
Friday	29/11/2013	32	2815	59932
Friday	29/11/2013	33	571	60503

And this is what they look like laid out in tables:

Words written over six days

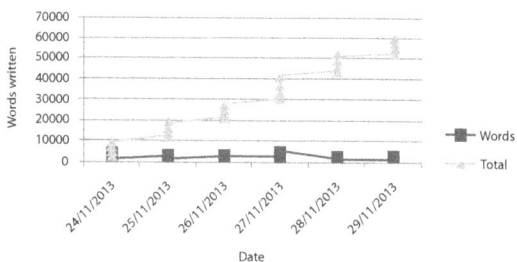

Words written per scene/chapter

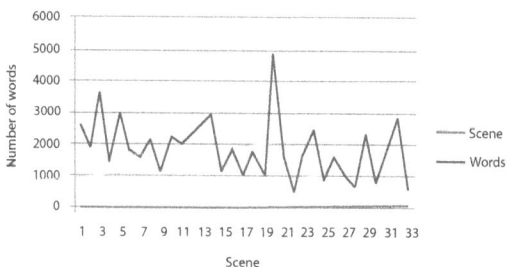

Words written per scene/chapter

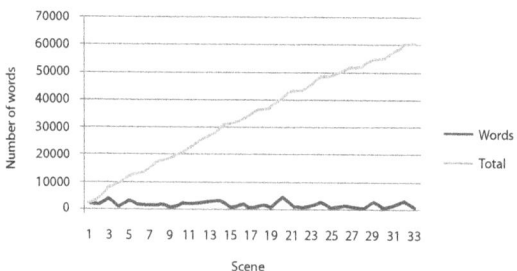

As you can see from the statistics, there was a definite dip on the third day. And then a peak on the fourth. The first and second days were still hopeful, although it was clear that speed and wordcount would be difficult. But I was averaging over 9,000 words a day, I was safe. The fifth and sixth days were exciting and energetic, I didn't want to stop as I realised I was going to make it – I was going to finish it and I was going to make my target of 60,000 words. The third and fourth days were difficult. Almost miserable.

TUES → WED

MIDWEEK MISERY

I wanted to be doing all the other things we could have done on a week away, I half resented the novel for taking me away from those things, I was struggling to write enough words per hour, I was struggling with the middle section of the book, all those loose ends that I thought I could tie up as I went along – it wasn't nearly so easy, I should have worked out what all those characters were doing and why before I started the pressurised writing part.

Sacrifice

If we go back to that list of ingredients I needed to write a book in less than a week, well one of them may be 'sacrifice'.

Just as no omelette is made without breaking eggs, so some things had to be lost so that my target could be gained.

I had to be prepared to give up some big pleasures so that I could achieve my goal.

I was on holiday in a beautiful place for a week, with gorgeous countryside roundabout, with a fabulous café across

WE'VE GOT TO BREAK SOME EGGS TO MAKE AN OMELETTE

the road, with my mum whose company I love – and I had to give it all up so that I could complete the novel. It was sitting there and I had to ignore it. That was what it was all about. I had to give up so many things I love doing on holiday, things like:

- spending time with mum
- going for walks
- enjoying exploring a new place
- painting ceramics
- hanging out in the café
- taking time over meals
- watching tv
- visiting the village's Jacobean stately home
- supper in a cosy corner of the local pub
- and lazing about reading books in front of the woodburner.

But it was a willing sacrifice. Because I wanted that end goal very much.

A sacrifice that I am happy to make doesn't feel so much like a sacrifice to me…it feels more like an energetic effort, an effort I am happy to put in because the end goal is something I really want and because the process can be enjoyable – even if it takes an effort. Often I *am* foregoing something, making a choice to do without something in my life, but it is a happy choice because there is joy in the effort, a sense of purpose in the hard work. The best analogy for me is the kind of effort and sacrifice we put into parenting – we are more than happy to go without all sorts of personal pleasures in order to do the best we can for our children, to spend time with them, to spend time, effort and thought on them. Perhaps this novel was one of my creative offspring.

Sacrifice isn't giving up something or going without: it's an exchange. We don't get something for nothing: if we gain on one level then we need

to give on another level. If I wanted to put energy into this book, then I wouldn't have energy to give to other pursuits.

I had warned myself and mum that I wouldn't have time for anything but writing during our week in Derbyshire – I had paved the way.

I had sorted the family out in advance so I wouldn't have to worry about anyone or anything except writing for the whole time I was away – I even sorted out every aspect of my 50th birthday celebrations, to happen on the weekend after our writing week.

When I left the cottage on the Saturday morning of my 50th birthday, I had spent a week writing – and had done very little else. I hadn't had a conventional week's holiday, I hadn't really appreciated my surroundings much, I hadn't spent much quality time with my mum – just the occasional half hour between bursts of writing, I hadn't relaxed much, in fact much of the time I had been under quite a lot of pressure, working hard, not stopping until I'd made my quota of words and sections. But I was happy. There wasn't a sense of going without. I didn't feel I'd missed out on things. I'd chosen not to do some things – and I'd come away with a finished novel. I was very happy.

Instead of 'sacrifice' I'm going to add 'effort' to the list of abstract ingredients I needed for writing my novel. Now my list looks like this:

1. **FAITH –** Belief in my ability

2. **LOVE –** Wanting to have a go

3. **SPACE –** Safe space to relax and be inventive

4. **SUPPORT –** Someone who understands and gives the right kind of support

5. **SHARING –** An audience, whether they give feedback or not

6. **EFFORT –** Being content to give up pleasures and put in the hard work

PART THREE – LEARNING
(FROM DOING)

The other day a writing friend said "You wrote a novel in a week? My goodness, how did you do it!"

"How did I do it?" I replied. Well, firstly:

1. I knew what I was doing ...

...and things are straightforward when you know what you're doing

and

2. I wanted to do it and I wanted to do it very much, in fact I wanted to do it enough to:

"What!?! you wrote a novel in a week?!?"

- overcome the obstacles
- push through the hard bits
- prepare a lot in advance
- practise
- set aside precious time
- spend money on it
- spend time and effort on it
- and go without pleasurable activities.

I've already expanded the list of ingredients I needed to write a novel in a week to six items:

1. FAITH

2. LOVE

3. SPACE

4. SUPPORT

5. SHARING

6. EFFORT

and I can probably find more factors that helped and enabled me to write 60,000 words in six days.

Just as I could *expand* the idea of 'necessary ingredients', it is also possible for me to *reduce* the whole enterprise to two essential factors –

I knew what I was doing and I wanted to do it very much.

I had knowledge and desire, otherwise known as ability and motivation or 'can' and 'will'.

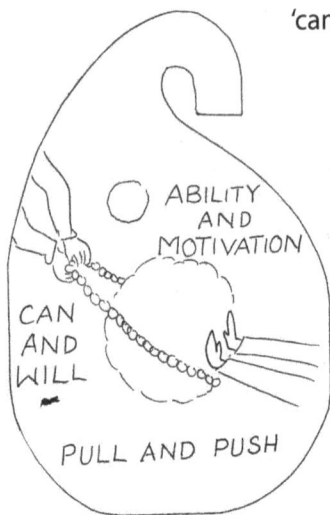

If knowledge is power, then desire could be the direction towards a goal, so my vehicle (the writing 'me') had fuel and direction – there was nothing holding me back.

The Knowledge

'It's easy when you know how.'

'It's easy when you know the answer.'

Ever watched a quiz show and called out a few answers to a series of questions, when the contestants on the tv are struggling?

"Goodness, don't they know the answer!" you cry out. "It's easy!"

it's easy! (when you know the answer)

TV QUIZ

But of course it's only easy if you know the answer. If you don't know, then it isn't necessarily easy at all.

So in order for me to make it easier to write a 60,000-word story, I needed to know stuff – I needed to know all about the story, the characters, the setting, the events, the plot, the background. And I needed to know all about the practicalities of writing – some basic grammar, punctuation, spelling, sentence structure, dialogue, description. I needed to know how to use my laptop, and the software. And how to type. I also needed to know that I could physically write 1,000 words in an hour. Just so that I knew I would have enough hours in the day to get it done.

I was armed with this knowledge when I started writing.

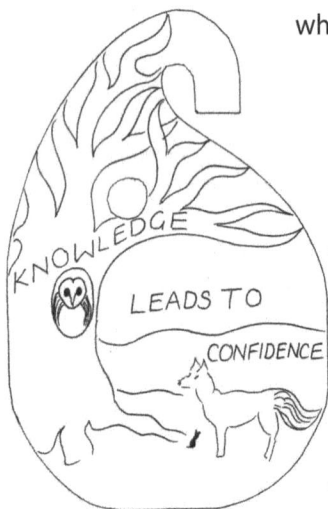

This kind of knowledge gives confidence.

Planning and prep-aration, research and learning, are essential for this kind of knowledge. There have been fabulous novels written by young people, by people who have had little formal education, and by people who haven't read all the classics, so these don't make proper excuses not to try. You do, however, need to do at least some preparation and planning, I have found out.

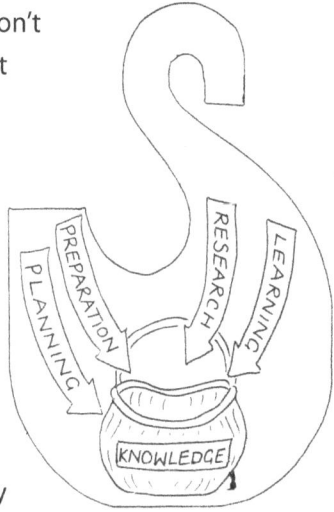

And this is where I'll put my hand up and admit 'the six-day story' is really a bit of a misnomer.

Because although I *wrote* it in a week, I did prepare it on and off, here and there, for several months beforehand.

But this is a book about completion – it's about what I've learnt from writing a novel in less than a week.

Perhaps one of the things I've learnt, from writing the novel and from life, is that the things that *appear easy* have often taken a good deal of hard work behind the scenes.

Think of the experienced actors in a smooth performance on stage – and then think of the many months of rehearsals and learning lines, and stagehands making scenery, and the designers and the costume-makers, and the lighting engineers, and the front of house staff, all of whom have gone into making that one night at the theatre appear so easy and effortless.

BEHIND THE SCENES

Think of the sportsmen and women and their many hours of practice and training for just an hour on the pitch. I have lived with a son who was a professional sportsman, so I know how very many hours of training they put in.

I've also found sometimes that the effort, the hard work, can be going on in my subconscious and lead up to a result that appears easy at the end.

It was like this when I stopped smoking (2006) and when I stopped drinking (2008).

Once I got to the moment I stopped it was easy, it really was. There was no effort involved, there was no will power necessary, I just plain stopped. I'll tell you why it was easy – because all the hard work had been going on in my head over the years beforehand. Drip, drip, drip, the reasons to stop had worn away at my excuses for continuing over many years. All the times that I'd gone for a run and stopped for a cigarette half way round and thought 'this is daft, why am I doing a healthy thing like running to get fitter and still smoking at the

same time?'; all the times I'd thought what a poor example I was setting to my children; all the times I wanted to take better care of myself, that I deserved better care; all the times I felt depressed the day after drinking, when I regretted poor decisions, foolish actions – over and over again. This is how and why regret can be useful. The messages in my head built up so eventually there was a tipping point – by the time I came to the day, the hour, the moment, then the moment of decision and the final action were easy.

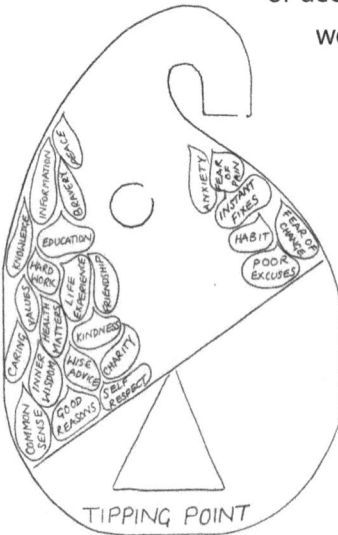

TIPPING POINT

Writing the novel was like that. Once it came to writing it, the pictures were so clear in my head, the people so real, the events so exciting, the places so tangible, that the words just flowed out of my fingers. They had been going on in my head for months before.

It's a bit like painting by numbers.

Do you remember painting by numbers?

When I was a child there were colouring books with pages divided into obscure black and white patterns, dozens of small sections with numbers in each one. It wasn't clear at first what the picture was going to be – it just looked like a mass of sections, all higgledy piggledy. But there was a key – for example, colour in all sections numbered 3 with brown, all sections numbered 6 with red, and so on. And if you followed the key, painting by numbers, when you got to the end the picture would be revealed – all the coloured sections joined up to make a coherent whole. The picture unfurled as you coloured it in.

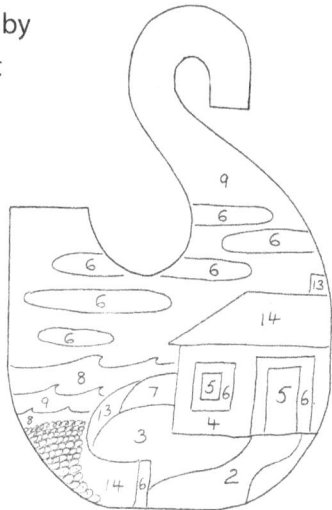

With the thirty sections of my story all plotted out, and with strong images of the characters and places in my head, when it came to writing the novel it was like painting by numbers – the plotted sections were the numbers, the characters and places were the colours, it was just a question of putting them together to make a whole picture.

When it came to putting pen to paper, I knew what I was doing.

The Motivation

The other essential factor was desire: *wanting* to write a whole story in a week.

If I hadn't really wanted to do it, it wouldn't have got done. Something would have cropped up, got in the way. I might have written a book one day, but I probably wouldn't have written one in a week. Or I might have spent a week writing but not quite finished a book.

There are many books written on motivation, you may have read some of them. Or better still, you may have analysed your own motivations and worked out what spurs you on and what slows you down. Self-knowledge is the best starting point.

I have a little pet diagram that I use when I try to describe how I see motivation.

Motivation is what gets us

from A → to → B

THE
MOTIVATION
EQUATION

A — STAY PUT — B

A — STAY PUT — B

A →→→→→ B MOVE

and in order for me to move from A to B, either B needs to seem fantastic to me in comparison to A, or A needs to feel terrible to me in comparison to B.

So if:

A = seems okay and B = seems okay

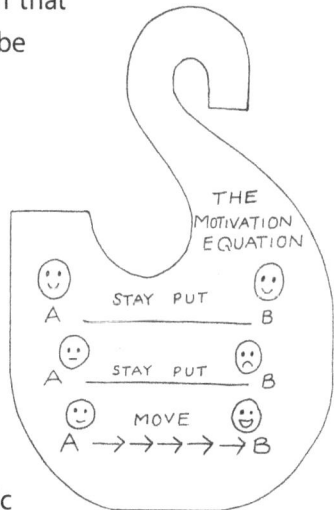

I won't be motivated to move, I won't want to change or to do something, because even though B is okay, A is also okay and I may as well stay at A. (Human beings don't really like making too much of an effort, if where we're at is alright we'll stay put – at least that's often how it is for me.)

Or if:

A = not much good but B = worse

I'll definitely stay put. This has sometimes been the case with jobs I've done: I've been a bit bored or disenchanted in one job, but being unemployed or in a worse job seems an awful idea so I've stuck with the job I've got.

Then again if:

A = okay but a bit dull and B = pretty
exciting

well then I'm definitely going to be tempted to move. This is the situation with where I live at the moment – there are many good things about where I live and I'm comfortable in my home, but when I see a property that inspires me or is in a different and new location, then I am often tempted to move house. (B hasn't moved me yet though, as A is just too okay to want to budge right now. It's summer as I write now and living in the country is lovely in the sunshine.)[7]

What I didn't realise to begin with, years ago, was that we can be more in control of our thoughts and feelings than we think we can. We often go along in a normal day having all those thoughts about our colleagues, and feeling all those emotions about the stresses of work or caring about our families, loving our homes or hating our jobs, liking cigarettes or wanting a glass of wine, and it may appear as if they just spring up and we can't do anything about them.

But that's not always true.

---

7 See After Words for an addition to the motivation equation.

WE ARE MORE IN CHARGE OF OUR MINDS THAN WE THINK WE ARE

BELIEFS

FEELINGS

THOUGHTS

we can choose what we put in our heads

but it's not easy to do

We can be more in control of our thoughts and feelings – if we want and if we try hard to achieve this control.

People who have struggled with addiction, with alcohol dependency, with behaviours or habits they have wanted to change, will know the sort of thing I'm talking about.

I'm not saying achieving control over our thoughts and feelings is easy, far from it, but I am saying it is possible. (There are many good books on this topic also, and many excellent counsellors, therapists, life coaches, and hypnotherapists, so I shall leave them to do their job and not go into it in too much depth here.)

And of course we have to really want to change in order to have the motivation to change some of these fundamentals about ourselves. That reminds me of the old joke:

Q. How many psychologists does it take to change a light bulb?

A. Only one, but the light bulb has to want to change.

Seriously, though, we need a lot of desire to change in order to see through the hard work of changing our thoughts and minds, some of those old patterns of thoughts and beliefs are pretty engrained.

It's not easy to change, but it is possible.

Once we admit it is possible to change our thoughts and feelings, then we can see that the motivation equation is easier to manipulate for us to achieve our goals.

Because we can choose what we put into the equation.

We are more in charge of our minds than we sometimes think we are.

For example, let's go back to me browsing property websites in the evening looking for the perfect property for me once all my children have left home and I am ready to downsize. If suddenly I lose my job and I have to move right now because I can't afford the house I'm living in, then it makes sense for me to concentrate on all the down points of where I live currently (it's so far from the shops, there's no public transport, I can't manage such a large house, the garden is separate from the house over a lane at the back, I'm a long way from groups and activities I'd like to be involved in) – this makes A look negative in my mind and I will find it easier to tear myself away from a nice house. And at the same time it would make sense for me to focus on all the good points of a move (it'll be a fun fresh start, I'll make money if I downsize, I can move to a town I'd like) – this makes B look more positive in my mind. Then I will be happy and motivated to move house.

On the other hand, if I find a job so I can afford the original old house and then the sale falls through on the new house and I'm left where I am, it then makes sense for me to reverse the thoughts I'm putting into my head – I'd count the blessings of living where I do (rabbits in the lane, birds in the trees, owls in the barn opposite, beautiful views) and that would help A feel better again so I wouldn't want to move so much.

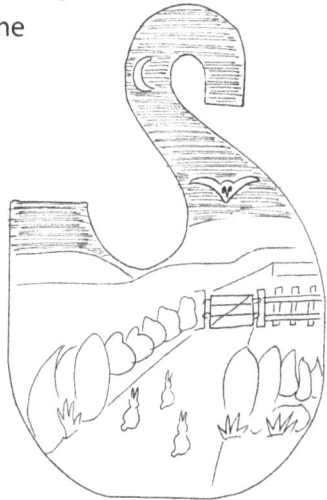

Flexibility

The key is flexibility of mind.

Being able to change from wanting one thing to being okay with what we've got.

Flexibility of mind is being able to switch the 'wanting' on and off, or at least being able to turn down the 'wanting' – like a volume button on the remote control. If we are in charge of what we want, when we want it, and how much we want it, and if we can turn down the 'wanting' when we've decided we no longer want to aim for that goal, well then this leaves us very free to choose how to be.

TURN DOWN
THE VOLUME
ON
'WANTING'

And in order to achieve this level of control over the 'wanting', we need to be more in control of our thoughts and feelings and we need to practise moving our thoughts and feelings around inside our mind. That way we get used to change as well.

I remember once a wonderfully inspiring thing I heard on the radio. A musician (I think) was talking about working with terminally ill people. There were people who faced cancer with a fighter's attitude, battling to beat the illness, struggling to stay alive, people who really *wanted* to live; then there were people who faced their illness with acceptance, they remained at peace with the thought of death, they were resigned to what would happen, they didn't *want* death but when it happened they would accept it. The radio presenter asked the musician a question: which way, did he think, was the best way to be when a person was diagnosed with a terminal illness? Was it better to try and fight the illness, to struggle? Or was it better to try and accept things and relax?

And the musician said that they had found that the people who managed terminal illness best were those who could switch swiftly between struggle and acceptance, back and forth.

Flexibility of mind, it is a great gift. It is not easy to achieve. We would need to practise flexibility of mind, as we would need to practise controlling our thoughts and feelings and what beliefs we put into our minds. My understanding is (and my personal experience has shown me) that good therapy, yoga, meditation and mindfulness can all help towards slowing down the pace of our thoughts so we have more control.

Music

Talking about the musician reminds me that, when I was writing my six-day story, music was part of my process.

I had my Ipod on shuffle connected to speakers in a different room, familiar songs but not loud enough to sing along with or to want to dance to – it was simply the semblance of a sound presence.

A little quiet music may not work for everyone, and certainly each of us will have our different tastes in music. But it was important for me not to have silence – silence would have been overwhelming, and I would have heard every creak in a spooky sixteenth-century cottage – and yet I didn't want to be distracted by anything where I could hear words, either loud music or speaking on a radio or tv. Hearing words would have interfered with the words I was putting on the page.

Incommunicado

There is something almost spiritual about shutting oneself away for a week to get something done. Mum and I made a writers' convent for two for a week.

A WRITERS' CONVENT

It was a special time. It had an intensity, not just because of the work I was doing, but also because we were separated from our normal lives and from the rest of the world.

But there was cosiness and comfort. The bubble I had made for myself was a delightful one, a cushioned cage, a luxurious cell. I was a prisoner by choice. I had created my own environment with a clear aim in mind, I was a hermit with a purpose.

Purpose

A sense of purpose is crucial.

It's hard to imagine how we would function as human beings without a sense of purpose. Other living creatures may have purpose and intention, but it seems as though we may be the only creatures who have a *sense* of purpose. When we lose our sense of purpose, how desolate that can be.

Previously I have been at the mercy of purpose. Purpose found me, captivated me. Other people set my targets, I responded by doing my best to achieve them – or sometimes rebelliously rejected them. My surroundings and cultural background devised me a purpose – as student, employee, traveller, partner, home-maker, mother. As various roles fell away – as the jobs changed, as the partner left, as the children grew up, as I changed my mind – my purpose changed. What was I? Where was I going? What was I going to do with my life? And, most importantly (it seemed to me at the time), why?

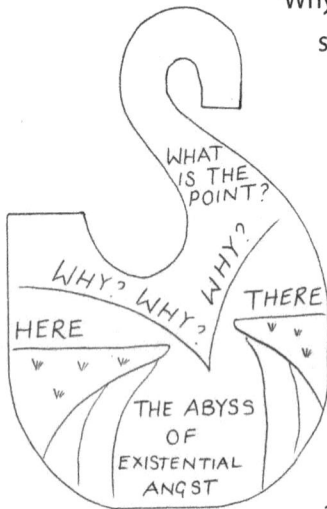

'Why?' is one of the biggest scariest questions, I have found. Particularly when I have applied it to me. A wise life coach I once visited a few times advised me to avoid the question 'why?' She was right. Asking 'why?' has sometimes led me into deep, depressing existential angst.

As I ploughed my way out of those depths a few years ago, a little bit of Buddhism (or more likely a lot), mixed with some phrases I remembered from some Muslim friends 20 years ago, helped me soften into a greater acceptance of 'things as things be' rather than trying desperately to find reasons for existence.

When my children were tiny we lived in the centre of Leeds and I started learning Urdu, it was on offer at a community centre near us. There were two phrases in Urdu that have remained with me across the years: *Insh'allah* and *Mash'allah*.

Insh'allah إن شاء اللّٰه

Mashallah ما شاء اللّٰه

Insh'allah means 'if God wills it' and *mash'allah* means 'thanks be to God'.[8]

---

8   I have since found out that 'Mash'allah' may be translated as 'God has willed it so'. However, this was not the translation I was given originally and it was not the message I carried with me. In my head, the phrases 'if it be so' and 'thanks be' were the messages that worked for me.

These phrases helped me with acceptance. If you don't believe in God, you can turn the phrases into 'if it be so' and 'thanks be' – these are messages to the soul to relax, to accept, to roll with how things are, and then to be grateful.

As I have mellowed in to middle age, I have learnt to make purpose work for me in a healthier way than I did before.

In the past I have been afraid of the purpose gap. I have been running scared from the absence of an answer to the 'why' question. I have been so scared of the purpose gap that I have filled it with all sorts of unhealthy things, in a desperate attempt not to look into the gap where I wanted meaning to be.

OTHER PEOPLE'S PURPOSE GOALS
Do good
Be a good mother
Be a good student
Get a good job
Keep the family together
Be happy
Do something worthwhile
Please people
Make a home
Achieve
work hard

Probably my first biggest purpose filler was my long-term partner. Being with him was my purpose, and I dedicated myself to that. Then along came the children, and I joyously gave myself over to looking after them – they became my purpose. And I don't think this is necessarily a bad thing when it comes to parenting. I certainly could not have done a half-way decent job of bringing the children up without dedicating myself to that task. But our role as parents shifts as our children get older – purpose is not static.

Combining partner and children meant that the family became my purpose; when my partner left and our family structure reconfigured at the same time my sense of purpose also left for a while – if family had been my goal and the family was broken, then I had clearly failed. That was my thinking in those days. In the miserable moments, vodka,

FILLING THE PURPOSE GAP WITH UNHEALTHY BEHAVIOURS

HERE I AM BUT...

SELFISH CHILDISH DISCO DANCING GOING OUT BEING SILLY NIGHT CLUBS THOUGHTLESS QUICK FIXES ROMANCE CHOCOLATE VODKA

...WHERE AM I GOING?

chocolate, cigarettes, night clubs, unsuitable romances and irresponsible behaviour all failed to fill the purpose gap.

More recently as my children grew up and began to leave home, I have floundered about thinking I should find a new career, a new house, a new start, a new reason for me.

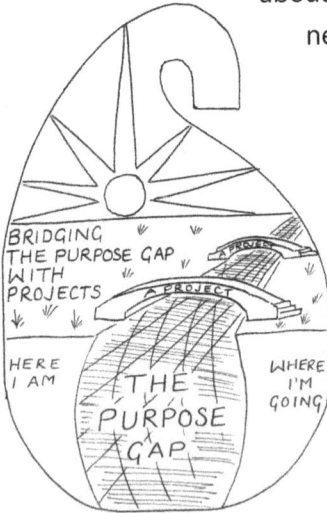

BRIDGING THE PURPOSE GAP WITH PROJECTS

A PROJECT

HERE I AM

THE PURPOSE GAP

WHERE I'M GOING

My most recent solution to coping with the purpose gap is to approach purpose on a daily basis with small projects.

This feels much more within my control – I have not handed over my purpose for existence to anyone else, or to a career that someone else could alter. It is more reliable than unsuitable romances, and a lot healthier than vodka, chocolate and cigarettes.

Now I find enough purpose to delight me in small projects.

Instead of one overarching reason for my existence as there was in the past, like an enormous job title balanced on my head: COUNSELLOR – MOTHER – PARTNER – PROBATION WORKER – PARTY PERSON – PERFECTIONIST – PET-OWNER, now there are a million small reasons for me to be me, for me to be in this world.

One big reason for my existence?

PERFECTIONIST

WORKER

MOTHER

One day my purpose might be to listen to a friend over coffee, the next day I will find purpose in designing letter paper for my aunt; one weekend I will be driven by a project

A million small reasons for me to be me

THINGS TO MAKE

BOOKS TO WRITE

IDEAS TO RESEARCH

DRESSES TO MAKE

to make a kitten playbox out of a laundry box, the next I will have an idea for adding a Jean-Paul Gaultier neckline to the standard tunic dress I wear to work; one autumn I will plan to write a novel in a week, the next spring I'll be writing the book about how I did it.

For me, now, purpose is a project. Or perhaps I should put it the other way round – each project is purpose, it brings its own purpose with it, it fills me with purpose.

My gran used to say about children: 'they come and they bring their loaf with them' – I guess she meant that (amazingly and most of the time) we manage to find what we need to sustain our children even if we feel we won't be up to the task.

If projects can be seen as creative offspring in a way, then we could say about projects: 'they come and they bring their purpose with them'.

And the joy of projects is that they are within my control. On my own, in the dining room of an old cottage in a Derbyshire village, miles from anywhere, out of touch with my friends and family, with only the means to write and draw alongside me, I created a sense of purpose for myself.

This has given me freedom. I am no longer dependent on others for feeling purposeful. Jobs, friends, partners, houses, careers, pets, interests, passions may come and go, even my children will breeze in and out of my life as they grow up and go on out into the world, but as long as I have a mind to have an idea and my hands to make it, then I know I can create that sense of purpose wherever I am.

Rather than expecting other people, jobs, places, to make me happy, I now make my

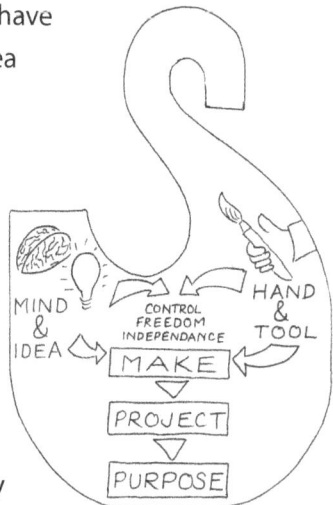

MIND & IDEA

HAND & TOOL

CONTROL
FREEDOM
INDEPENDANCE

MAKE

PROJECT

PURPOSE

own happiness on a daily basis by creating my own projects.

Purpose is a project.

Projects make purpose.

Goals

Each project probably needs a rough idea of an end goal. So that we know when the project is completed. And so we have a sense of direction and motivation.

As with plans, I think it can be useful to be flexible about goals – we can be as fixed and focussed or as easy-going as we need or want to be.

So if a project calls for a clear goal, a measurable specific outcome at a given time – then we can plan and work towards that. If a project is more experimental, if the goal is more about what we are learning through the process and the practice, then we can afford to be a little more vague.

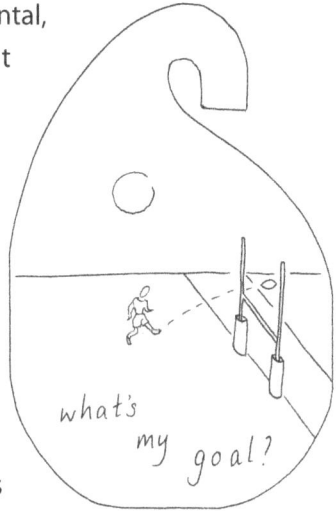

what's my goal?

For me with the book-in-a-week project, it was crucial that I was clear with myself that the end goal was about **finishing a 60,000-word story in a week.**

At various times I would find myself getting side-tracked, wanting to write a better novel, wanting to spend more time on various aspects, characterisation or dialogue, for example.

This is where the solid supporter comes in handy.

This is where I needed to be reminded that the goal was *finishing it*.

It didn't matter whether it was any good. Writing good prose was not my goal.

It didn't matter if it was a daft plot, melodramatic and over-complicated.

It didn't matter if all the loose ends weren't tied up.

It didn't matter if no one beyond my devoted family ever read it.

The only thing that mattered was finishing.

And the wordcount, of course.

Because without it being 60,000 words long, it wouldn't feel like a book to me.

So I had twin inter-related goals.

On the motivation from A → to → B diagram, it would have looked like this:

STATE A ⇒ STATE B

No finished novel ⇒ Finished novel

Dissatisfied ⇒ Satisfied

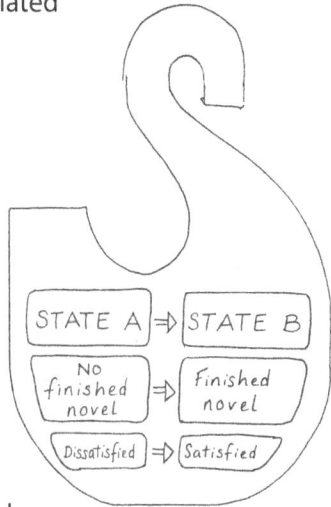

(This pre-supposes that a story of 60,000 words qualifies as a novel, which may be debateable…)

If this is a book about completion, about finishing, about achieving my goal, how did I do that?

How did I achieve my goal?

I have a feeling there are several different ways of looking at how I achieved my goal.

We've already looked at a couple.

There was the recipe of ingredients:

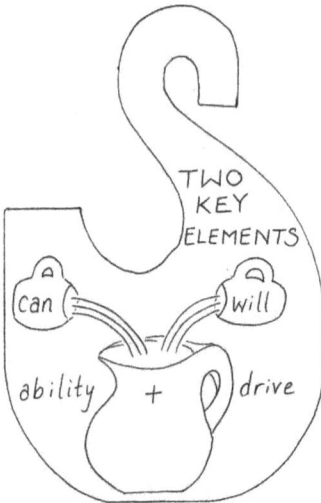

1. FAITH
2. LOVE
3. SPACE
4. SUPPORT
5. SHARING
6. EFFORT

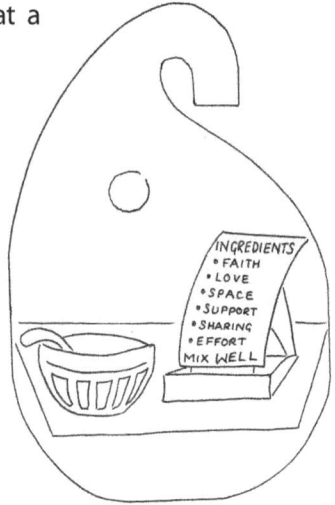

And there was the two key elements:

I knew what I was doing and I wanted to do it very much.

They equate to 'can' and 'will', ability and drive, knowledge and motivation.

To these perspectives, I could also add:

IDEA→DESIRE→PREPARE→ALLOCATE TIME AND SPACE→DO IT

Which could also be called:

SEED→MOTIVATION→PLAN→PRACTICALITIES→ACTION

If we wanted to look at it in another way, we could say:

Define your goal → visualise the benefits → be specific about the details → keep your vision in mind → while you take steps towards your goal

And if we're to follow the lead from sports people and other professionals, we would put the following into action:

OBSERVE→ PRACTISE→KNOW WHAT I'M DOING→DO IT

And I could also say that in order to achieve my goal, I needed:

a. Realism

b. Clarity

c. An overview

I bet we could make a motivational self-help book out of any of the above models. If you look on the shelves of the bookshop, you can find plenty of books about goals – setting goals, working towards goals, achieving goals. There are dozens of different models.

There are also plenty of life coaches (and sports coaches, career coaches, NLP and CBT practitioners, and so on) all of whom are trained to help us achieve our goals.

Perhaps the best I can say is that there are many different ways of looking at our goals and how we can best achieve them. Some models work for some people in some situations. You will find what works best for you.

Getting Told v. Being Offered

I don't like to be told how to do things.

Does that make me sound very stroppy? Perhaps I am.

I don't mean that I don't ever want to be told anything. I often want to be told things and I will go out of my way to find the right advice at the right time, to seek out the best teacher, to look for the kind of instruction I need or want.

But I don't like to be told things when I haven't asked for help.

BOSSY BOOTS

"you don't want to do it like that!"

Maybe a psychologist would suggest I am stuck in a rebellious teenage phase.

Perhaps I am exploring a new-found independence.

I was a very 'good girl' when I was young, I did as I was told and handed my homework in on time. Was this the fall-out from being a first child? The early stages of perfectionism?

This latest stage of my life has allowed me the freedom to learn in a different way – rather than being instructed by people, I prefer to explore and experiment.

Feeling my way in the dark

This does mean that I bump into the furniture a good deal (metaphor-ically), because I am feeling my way in the dark sometimes, but it also means that I learn a lot. And it feels as if I am learning more because of the bumping and bruising than I did when I did what I was told.

We can't follow this 'learning through trying' method for everything in life, it would be too risky. Well, we can, but if we do then we risk being hurt a good deal. We can't keep touching all those ovens to find out just how hot they are without getting burnt much of the time.

do I need to touch the oven to find out it's hot?

Some people sometimes appear to be learning the hard way over and over again, and it can be frustrating to watch to say the least. If we care about the individuals involved, then it can be agonising to watch our friends and family risk their health and safety because they won't listen to advice or prefer to follow their own path.

I don't want to upset or worry my family and friends. I've probably done enough of that in the past.

So I try to keep my experiential learning to the arts and crafts and creative fields now.

I have experimented with other things – I worked in a post office for a day, I have had a dog for a weekend, I completed half a psychology A level and half a counselling degree, I have had a building survey completed on a hairdressers I was considering investing in, I rented a workshop for a year, I did three months of night shifts, and so on.

I called my experiments 'thistles'. There is a chapter in Winnie the Pooh, 'in which Tigger comes to the forest and has breakfast'.[9] Tigger is a big enthusiast. When Pooh invites him to breakfast and asks if he likes honey, Tigger tells Pooh that Tiggers like everything. Little by little Tigger discovers that he doesn't

9   *The House at Pooh Corner*, by A. A. Milne. 1928, Methuen, London.

like the honey that Pooh Bear eats and he doesn't like the 'haycorns' that Piglet eats and he doesn't like the thistles that Eeyore eats. Tigger thinks he likes all these things to eat but it's only when he tries them that he realises he doesn't like them at all. He had to learn the hard way.

Tiggers don't like thistles...

I learnt a good deal from my thistles, but they cost me in time, money and energy. Fortunately they did not cost me in health or sanity – or at least not too much.

But experiments in life can be costly.

There are consequences from all our actions. Even if we can't foresee what they will be at the time.

So when I say I don't like being told, I am talking about the field of creativity.

I would, for example, prefer to mess around with paint in my workshop than to do an Arts Foundation course at the moment. As and when I want to learn a specific technique, then I will enquire at the local college.

Help is helpful when we need it, but not when we don't.

"want this?"   "oh thanks!"

HELP

ONLY
HELP IS HELPFUL
WHEN WE DECIDE
WE WANT IT

Being a grown up with a mind of my own I would prefer to ask when I can't manage something, rather than having help thrust upon me.

My point is:

It's great when advice is offered, (particularly if we have asked for help); but it is not great when we are told there is a 'right' way to do something.

So it is with achieving goals.

So it is with writing a novel in a week.

If I told you there was one way to write a novel and a 'right' way to write a novel in a week, I would not be helpful to you.

I would also be wrong.

What I am trying to do in this book is describe what I have done and what I have learnt from it.

Okay, so I've had a few thoughts along the way about how I might be able to apply what I've learnt to other things – could I use the same methods I used to write a novel in a week to achieve other goals? Maybe I could.

But also I could probably use other methods effectively too.

What I hope is that there are some parts of this book that make you think 'aha' – either you recognise something you already do, or you see something you'd like to try, or you think you'd better steer clear of something else – some small gain.

Even if you think, 'well I knew all that already', then that's great because it's confirming we're both bright enquiring humans coming to similar conclusions.

Even if you think, 'that's a load of tosh', well that's not a bad thing because even negative information is useful. Just like me finding out that I don't want to work in a post office or that having a new dog is a bit like having a new baby (they can both be quite needy). Even negative information is information, and information is useful.

"That's Your Opinion!"

"That's your opinion, mum!" – says my youngest son to me (frequently), meaning basically 'you are speaking for yourself and not for me', 'that's how you feel about it, and it doesn't necessarily apply to everyone'.

"that's your opinion, Mum"

And he is, of course, correct.

When I speak it is only my opinion. I cannot claim to speak for anyone apart from myself.

I can observe other people and make some reasonable guesses about life and human beings from what other people do, and I can ask other people about their experiences, and I can read and research about people and life and psychology.

But what I can't do is take one instance of my experience and draw conclusions about the rest of humankind from that.

My son is right to warn me against this.

I am quick to go from personal experience to intellectual abstraction – what overall human truth can be extracted from my immediate experiencing and observing of the world? This can be interesting but it can also be a burden and I have to be aware of this habit of mine to prevent it obscuring what I see and what I learn.

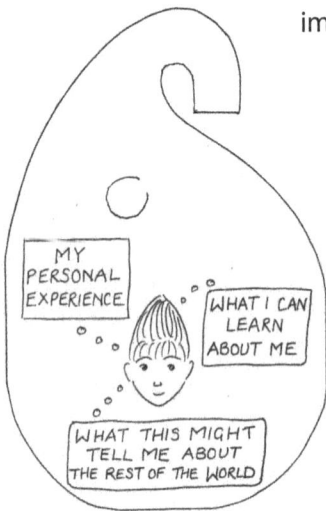

MY PERSONAL EXPERIENCE

WHAT I CAN LEARN ABOUT ME

WHAT THIS MIGHT TELL ME ABOUT THE REST OF THE WORLD

It would be no help to you if I said "I wrote a novel in a week, and I did it this way, so therefore that means that all people are able to write a novel in a week if they do it this way".

That would be a bit like giving you an instruction.

A bit like 'telling' not 'showing'.

But it might just be interesting to you if I *offer* you a description of what I have done in order to write a novel in a week and the personal conclusions I have come to in the process.

the tea of techniques

" fancy this? "

the cake of motivation

What works for me will not necessarily work for another person – and it may not work for me next time either.

On the other hand, parts of this *might* work for you, and I *might* be able to write another novel this autumn by using the same techniques.

Take what you will from this and move on.

What Works?

'What works' used to be a phrase bandied about in the probation service a few years ago. I believe it was to do with basing probation practice on techniques and processes that had been proven to reduce re-offending. The evidence was provided by psychological studies, research and statistics.

This kind of 'what works' is not foolproof – the statistics may show that one technique is more likely to prevent re-offending, data may show that a certain intervention is more helpful than others, but nothing is guaranteed.

So I can't say what works.

I can just say what did work for me, that one time.

If I do it again this year, and then maybe again next year…

If I find I can apply my methods to other goals I want to achieve in my life…

If you contact me and say you tried to apply similar methods and you achieved similar things…

If we run a study…

Well then, we can maybe begin to make a theory out of it.

Until then, it is safer for me to say, this is what I did and this is how it turned out.

So for me, on reflection, this is what worked last year when I wanted to write a novel in a week:

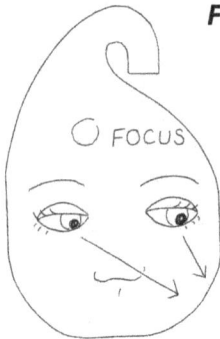

Focus – I excluded distractions, and pared life down to a minimum – we had only simple pleasures, an almost monastic existence, ascetic, frugal – the opposite of hedonism, the opposite of pleasure-seeking; all my energy was focussed in one direction.

Commitment – and accountability – I had a personal contract with myself and tied my supporters into this.

Provision – I had comfort and encouragement – I had Maslow's hierarchy of needs well covered.[10]

---

10 *Motivation and Personality*, by Abraham H. Maslow. 1954, Harper, NY.

Preparation – I had done my planning; I had my route map, and now could concentrate on 'painting by numbers'.

Practice – I had carried out my tests, I knew I could do it; I had some basic writing experience – this gave me both realism and confidence.

And I had my essential ingredients:

1. **FAITH –** Belief in my ability

2. **LOVE –** Wanting to have a go

3. **SPACE –** Safe space to relax and be inventive

4. **SUPPORT –** Someone who understands and gives the right kind of support

5. **SHARING** – An audience, whether they give feedback or not

6. **EFFORT** – Being content to give up pleasures and put in the hard work

Reflecting on what works for me, I recognise the importance of setting. Previously I have noted that I would rather not stop for a cup of tea if I can't find a café with the atmosphere I'm after, and after writing a novel in a week I know one of the factors was that mum and I managed to create the right atmosphere for me to work in. A room of one's own, yes, but not just any old room for me – it's possible I may not be able to finish things without the right place to do it in.

THE IMPORTANCE OF SETTING

Sharing is like therapy. It is the thought that I am going to share something that makes me think about it differently and choose my words more carefully; like therapy too, when I read it out loud to the writing group, I can hear my words back at me, and I'm not always comfortable with what I hear.

The process of reflection is a powerful thing.

what do my words sound like?

SOUNDING BOARD

Focus

I find it easier to focus on one thing at once.

Equally, if I have only one main *effortful* thing to do in the day then I am more likely to get it done and less likely to dread the task. There is something about single-mindedness that works for me. Similarly, I am sure I only got a good degree because I was (fortunate enough to be) able to concentrate entirely on studying in my final year, whereas my friends divided their attention between studying, working part-time behind the union bar, learning to drive, searching for a job, looking for a soul-mate, or coping with crazy boyfriends.

A single-minded focus doesn't work for everyone, we are all different. Other people appear to multi-task with great joy; they love to have many plates spinning and also manage to finish projects when they have several on the go. I have discovered I am not like this. Yes, I can carry out several simple things at once, or I can be doing a job on auto-pilot (the washing up perhaps) and keep the forefront of my mind clearly focussed on, say, the conversation I am having with my daughter on skype. This kind of domestic multi-tasking is not a problem for me. Perhaps parenting small children gets us in practice for doing a few mundane tasks while keeping

MULTI-TASKING
juggling
and
spinning plates

our attention on the important people in our lives.

But when it comes to bringing the thoughtful bits of my mind to a subject, and when it comes to getting bigger things finished, then I need to focus. Personally, I would prefer to get a training course finished in six months and do nothing but that, rather than doing it part-time over a year or two while working. As I have discovered with the courses and studying I have engaged in over the last few years, I lose steam if I split my focus.

And so it was with the novel. I had never finished a long story prior to this one because I'd never focussed entirely on finishing one – to the exclusion of everything else.

Momentum

Why this method worked for me, and why previous methods haven't worked for me, comes down to a combination of factors –

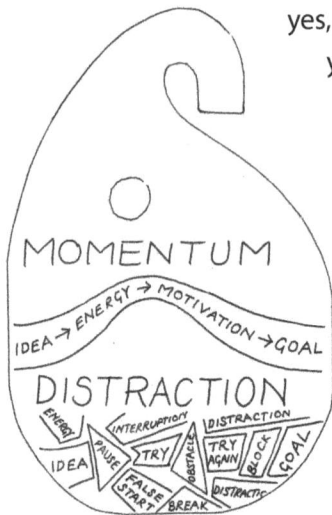

yes, planning, yes, a clear goal, yes, distraction-free space, but also momentum.

It's not possible to run a mile in 100-yard chunks.

We can do – but if we do, then it isn't a whole mile we've run, it's a series of 100-yard sprints. It's different. If I pause and hold on to the edge of the pool after each length I've swum, then I won't have swum a quarter of a mile, I will have swum several dozen lengths.

So it has been with me writing previously. When I have broken stories down into chunks and tried to write a few pages or a chapter here or there in amongst the rest of my life, it has been like running a mile in chunks. There are too many gaps where life wriggles in between. It's too easy to go off and do other things. I forget where the story was up to. I have to reread it to remember, and then when I reread it I become critical and want to change it or don't want to continue.

I lose momentum.

I lose the thread and inspiration.

I lose continuity.

Yes, writing a novel in a week isn't an easy way to do it, but it was possibly the best way for me to do it then.

I haven't written this book I'm writing now in a week – it's taken me a few months, and I've drifted in and out of it. But I bet the best bits of it have been written all at once – when I had that momentum, when the idea was flowing in me.

When I came to read back the novel I wrote in a week, it wasn't all that bad. There were patches that didn't quite work for me, there were some clichés and patches of melodrama that might be a little embarrassing, there were some twists of the plot that I could have worked out better, and I would very much like to improve my style. But it worked as a whole. It had a wholeness about it, a smoothness, a continuity, a flow – something I don't believe it would have had if I'd been stop-starting it.

I admire writers who can leave stories and come back to them and pick up where they left off. I'm not sure I can do that – yet.

The story and the characters and most of all the images, the locations, the actions, the scenes, all existed vibrantly, vividly in my head for that week. Their vivacity, their colours might have dimmed or altered (corrupted? faded? weathered?) if I had left them for any length of time. That was what had happened previously with stories I'd tried to write. The images had faded, the momentum had slowed down, the fire had cooled. That's why I had half a dozen unfinished novels and first chapters of stories lying around on the metaphorical top shelves of my mental storage shed.

I've described how I achieved a good degree by not focussing on other major distractions for four years. I'm pretty certain that if I wanted to study or re-train now I would have to give up work and focus only on my training in order to do well.

I now think that my personality works best at a subject when I am able to focus on it to the exclusion of other things. This is why the novel-in-a-week method worked for me. It might not be so great for you. That's fine. We're all different. But try it and see. If you want to write a novel and haven't done so yet, it might work for you too.

I also think that I haven't got the patience to see out a three– or four-year degree course as I had in my youth. I think three or four years would allow me too much space to have other exciting and interesting distractions creep in and persuade me to go off in other directions. Limitations appear to work for me.

There we are about to write a novel, embarking on a creative project that demands imagination and an open-mind and I am recommending limits, boundaries, structure, going without, and self-denial. It seems contradictory. But it worked for me. By limiting and reducing all the rest of my life down to one thing – writing – it opened up the horizons inside my head.

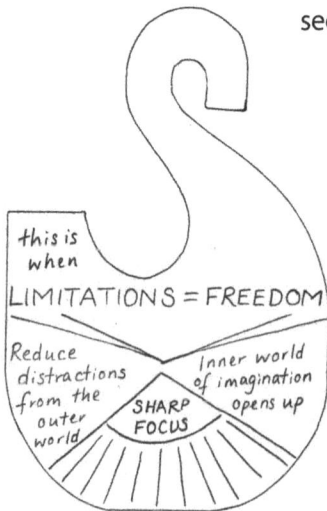

this is when

LIMITATIONS = FREEDOM

Reduce distractions from the outer world

SHARP FOCUS

Inner world of imagination opens up

For the six-day story, I kept the momentum going by reducing the time span and limiting distractions. I don't think I would have finished the novel otherwise.

Limits, Pressures and Priorities

This brings me on to what Eldar Shafir and Sendhil Mullainathan call 'scarcity'.[11] In the book of that name, they explain that scarcity 'captures the mind' so that when we feel poor in something – if we are short of money, or time, for example – then we can think of little except this lack. This excessive concern with our lack of something damages our ability to function well. It is a fascinating book and easy to read for something with such big thoughts in it and I would do it a disservice if I tried to summarise their ideas here. Suffice to say that we can see how, if we have a lot of something, we may become careless with it, we may not use it well, and if we have less of something important it may become more precious to us and we may take great care how we spend it.

The book concentrates mainly on the negative consequences of scarcity. But one

---

11   *Scarcity: why having too little means so much*, by Sendhil Mullainathan and Eldar Shafir, published by Allen Lane, London, 2013.

of the good results of scarcity is focus – something they call the 'focus dividend'. And Mullainathan and Shafir use the writing deadline as an example. "Once the lack of time becomes apparent, we focus," they write. "Picture yourself writing a book. Imagine that the chapter you are working on is due [with your editor] in several weeks. You sit down to write. After a few sentences, you remember an e-mail that needs attention. When you open your in-box, you see other e-mails that require a response. Before you know it, half an hour has passed and you're still on e-mail." They continue to describe how easy it is to be distracted and how very little writing gets done that day. "Now imagine the same situation a month later. The chapter is due in a couple of days, not in several weeks. This time when you sit down to write, you do so with a sense of urgency. When your colleague's e-mail comes to mind, you press on rather than get distracted. And best of all, you may be so focussed that the e-mail may not even register. Your mind does not wander to lunch [...] By day's end this focus pays off: you manage to write a significant chunk of the chapter."[12]

My youngest son, who is quick to admit he is not the most focussed student, recently said that he was going to ask his teachers not to give him such long deadlines to do his work – he was sure that if pieces of work *had* to be in on a Monday he would do them over the weekend, whereas if he is allowed to hand them in at the end of the month he leaves them until the last minute.

I can relate to this and I think my son's strategy is a good one. Yes, sometimes we can be very self-disciplined and get into the habit of doing something regularly – going for a run before work, clearing up ingredients as we go along when we are cooking, switching

---

12   Mullainathan and Shafir, 2013: 22.

off the tv and getting to bed early, getting our homework done as soon as it is set – but other times we may find it really difficult to do the things we know we should do (and also often really want to do) and that's when we can draft in help and support.

Going to personal trainers, life coaches, evening classes are some of the ways we oblige ourselves to stick with something we want to have in our lives. As a result of writing the novel in a week and then starting this book, I have become involved in setting up a writing group at our local library – I wanted something that would *make* me write fiction on a regular basis.

When I went away to try to write a book in a week, I was employing an external mechanism to create an internal pressure. The isolation and the timeframe were a self-imposed scarcity in order to provide a distraction-free intensely focussed atmosphere that I am not able to create at home. I can understand why some artists and writers walk to an office in a separate place from their home. I do have a workshop in our summerhouse in the garden, but I know that if I tried to set it up as a writing room I would easily become distracted by bits of gardening, or getting the washing in, or sorting my boxes of fabric. And every time I came in to get a cup of tea I would no doubt find another domestic chore that 'needed' to be done before teatime. And then of course at home there is the phone…and emails…and the internet…and the post… and the neighbours…and the family…all of which provide such delightful distractions.

WRITER DISTRACTED BY THE GARDEN

Which is why the self-imposed isolation of the week away worked so well – no signal for our mobiles, no landline, no internet connection, no post, no family, no neighbours.

And the very limited amount of time available meant I *had* to keep focussed.

I have considered what might have happened if I'd had eight days to write a novel, not six. Or what if I'd had ten days? Or two weeks not one? What do you think? I am pretty certain that a longer period of time might have been worse for me. Okay, so maybe eight days not six would have been pleasant, as I could have taken a longer lunch-break and had a walk round the village with mum. But any longer than eight days and I think the distractions would have crept in. Writing a book in a week worked for me not just because there was just enough time – but because there wasn't any time to do anything but write. So I had to focus. I had to write every waking minute for ten hours a day at a rate of 1,000 words an hour. And I couldn't afford to do anything else.

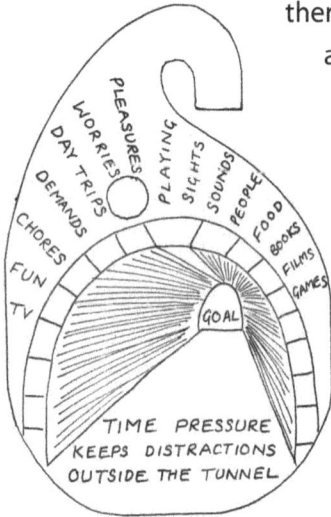

The time pressure forced all possible distractions out of the way.

Priorities

If I had gone away to write for two weeks and had allowed myself to write in the morning and visit the surrounding area in the afternoon, I don't think I would have got the book completed. Or if I had finished the book, I'm not sure I would have done as good a job. I might have waffled more. I might have tinkered with the plot more. I might have altered things mid-story. I might have found something in the village that I wanted to write about more, or something I wanted to do or visit. I might have felt I should make more effort to write a 'good' book or use 'better' style.

Half and half things, in my experience, often turn out to be neither one nor the other. So time away that was half for writing and half for holiday wouldn't have worked for me. I would have felt I hadn't done either one properly. I know this from all the times that I have tried to mix two priorities – when I split focus I feel as if I haven't really focussed on either. Sometimes I feel I have failed at both. For example, if I go away on holiday with the children, it is much better for me if I have only one main priority – spending time having fun as a family – rather than trying to incorporate visits to art galleries and museums and exhibitions. If I happen to have an afternoon on my own to wander round the local modern art gallery, then it is a bonus.

Going away to write a book in a week I had made my priorities clear – I was going away to write a 60,000-word story in six days, that was my number one priority, anything on top of that was a bonus.

Laziness v. Self-Control

Daniel Kahneman in his book *Thinking, Fast and Slow*[13] divides the way we think into two 'systems' – System 1: our automatic thinking system ('fast'), and System 2: deliberate thought that takes more effort ('slow'). The book is well worth reading. One of the earlier sections of the book describes how the mind will avoid making an effort if at all possible – which is why if we can get away with operating on auto-pilot then we will and why we have to push ourselves to pay attention and focus on things if we are tired. Kahneman describes how "switching from one task to another is effortful, especially under time pressure."[14] And explains that we "normally avoid mental overload by dividing our tasks into multiple easy steps [...] We cover long distances by taking our time and conduct our mental lives by the law of least effort."[15]

---

13   *Thinking, Fast and Slow*, by Daniel Kahneman, published by Penguin, London, 2011.
14   Kahneman, 2011: 37.
15   Kahneman, 2011: 38.

I am not a big fan of the word 'lazy'. It seems unnecessarily pejorative and judgemental. My experience has been that people usually throw the word 'lazy' at themselves or at other people when they feel they *should* have done or be doing something that they have not. My counter-argument is that there will be reasons why we have not mustered up the energy to carry out this duty we feel we *should* be doing. Maybe it's even possible that we don't really think we should be doing it and we have a legitimate case. Often it is my perception that some people label other people or certain behaviours as 'lazy' and it isn't fair – because we don't know everyone's back story, we can't say why they might put off doing something they should do: perhaps they have literacy difficulties so they struggle with forms so they don't fill them in; perhaps a friend or family member is suffering with illness or addiction so tidying the house up isn't a big priority.

And sometimes we are just plain downright exhausted.

People (myself included) so often forget tiredness.

TIRED (NOT LAZY)

LAZINESS = AVOIDING EFFORT
OFTEN FOR UNDERSTANDABLE REASONS

I wonder why I am more snappy in the evening – then I remember I got up at 6am for work. I wonder why I don't get round to seeing my friends over the Pennines in Leeds and Halifax, then I factor in that I am tired after a week of work and running the home and the family and I haven't the energy for a long day-trip. I wonder why I sit on the sofa and eat a whole tub of cookie dough ice cream at midnight, and then I realise I should have been in bed two hours earlier.

I am not lazy. I am hard-working. But I am also tired.

Tiredness and exhaustion can be the result of many things and they can take many forms.

Kahneman explains that we have limited resources of energy. This makes sense. Effort in one area means we will have less energy in another area: "...the transition to a faster walk brings about a sharp deterioration in my ability to think coherently,"[16] he explains.

He goes on to describe how "even in the absence of time pressure, maintaining a coherent train of thought requires discipline" and that "self-control and deliberate thought apparently draw on the same limited budget of effort".[17]

As Kahneman investigates further he discovers studies that prove that self-discipline appears to wear out with use and needs to be refreshed. "An effort of will or self-control is tiring; if you have had to force yourself to do something, you are less willing or less able to exert self-control when the next challenge comes around."[18] Which helps to explain my

---

16   Kahneman, 2011: 40.
17   Kahneman, 2011: 40.
18   Kahneman, 2011: 41.

eating the whole tub of Ben and Jerry's after a week of healthy eating.

Our self-discipline getting worn down in this way, Kahneman calls this 'ego depletion'. He describes how "ego depleted people [...] succumb more quickly to the urge to quit."[19]

I have long thought that it isn't possible to alter too many unhealthy habits all at once. Or rather, if you do try to stop smoking, cut down on alcohol, avoid sugar, go to the gym *and* eat more vegetables all at the same time, you'd better not have too many other priorities in your life because you won't have the energy to focus on them. And Kahneman's research appears to back this up.

WEARINESS (COMES FROM)

EFFORT EFFORT EFFORT
SELF-DISCIPLINE HARD WORK
EFFORT OF WILL EFFORT
EFFORT SELF-CONTROL
EFFORT EFFORT

---

19   Kahneman, 2011: 42.

On top of this, his studies show that mental faculties, and the slow-working deliberate thought of System 2, suffer if our energies are going elsewhere. I am less intelligent when my mind is trying to resist the tempting thought of ice cream.[20] It's worth remembering that we are all very individual when it comes to things we find effortful – one person may find it easy to socialise, for example, whereas for someone else a cocktail party may take a huge effort; one person might take to parenthood like a duck to water, whereas 24 hours a day nurturing a baby or toddler might take more effort for a different individual; some of us find sports easy, some of us are at ease in libraries, some of us like our own space and others find it a big effort to spend time alone. Those of us unaccustomed to public speaking or learning a foreign language may be surprised how exhausted we feel after a night on stage or a weekend abroad trying to converse in Spanish.

---

20 A similar point is made in *Scarcity* by Mullainathan and Shafir.

This brings me back to the beauty of the monastic lifestyle mum and I achieved in our writing cottage in Derbyshire – there was less for my mind to resist, fewer temptations, fewer distractions, fewer questions. I was free to use my mental energy for my number one priority – writing.

Routine and Habits

With my goal set, my priority in place, and my programme for each day carefully designed, there were no conflicts or questions in my mind – I didn't stop once to think, 'oh, should I take the afternoon off or should I really carry on writing?' There wasn't the problem of choice. I just had to stick with the programme.

In life I need a mixture of flexibility and routine. When it comes to getting something done, routine helps.

As you know, I hate someone else telling me what to do. But I'm a big fan of telling myself to do things.

And I do know that routine is good for two things:

a. instilling habits and

b. getting things done.

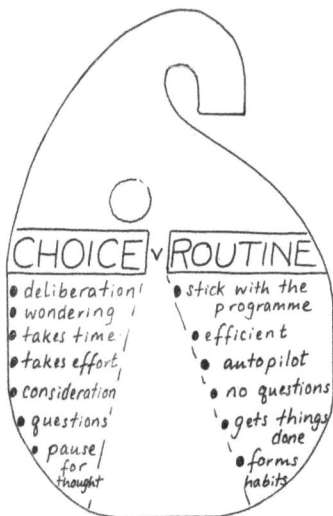

CHOICE v ROUTINE

- deliberation!
- wondering
- takes time
- takes effort
- consideration
- questions
- pause for thought

- stick with the programme
- efficient
- autopilot
- no questions
- gets things done
- forms habits

As a result of some of my experiences, I have thought a good deal about change, and how we can change ourselves, change our habits of thought and behaviour. I have learnt much about how I can change myself and I don't believe there is one foolproof way for me to fall back on every time. It's a bit like writing a novel in a week – there are some essential ingredients, and some helpful parameters, but no one-size-fits-all method.

Rock-paper-scissors

A month or two ago I developed an image I found helpful when I was thinking about change and habits.

I go swimming two or three times a week. On one of the days I go swimming I usually also see one of my closest friends for coffee (tea, actually). On this particular day a couple of months ago, as I was leaving the café with my friend she said: "I don't know how you can go swimming, I can't bear the thought of all the effort of getting cold and wet and then getting dry again and having to dry my hair and it all taking so long and being such a hassle."

I stopped and thought about what she had said. Paused just outside the café in the sunshine, I realised that what she described about swimming were my

cold + wet after swimming

SWIMMING POOL

thoughts about it too – I've always thought going swimming was a lot of hassle. Yes, I love it when I'm in the pool, and I love how I feel afterwards, but the palaver getting there and back and getting ready and getting wet and cold and then dry and warm again after, yes, it is an undeniable unenjoyable hassle. So if my thinking was the same as hers, why did I find it so *easy* to go swimming three times a week these days?

Then I realised.

I had got into the habit of it.

HABIT trumps HASSLE

You win!

HABIT

HASSLE

"I've just got used to it," I said to my friend. "I've got into the habit. And the habit sort of overcomes the hassle."

A few days later on I was in a Little Chef at the

services on the way to take my middle child back to uni.

I had my notebook out and was trying to illustrate the concept of 'habit overcoming hassle' – as you know, I like to be able to understand things visually.

"In the rock-paper-scissors of life, if 'habit' trumps 'hassle', what then trumps 'habit'?" I asked my son.

It didn't take him long to come up with the answer: "change", he said.

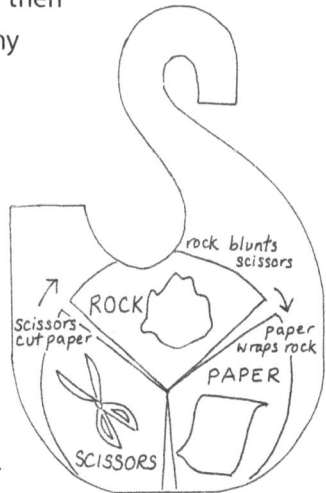

rock blunts scissors

ROCK

Scissors cut paper

paper wraps rock

PAPER

SCISSORS

So in the rock-paper-scissors of life, if 'habit' trumps 'hassle' (or rather 'perception of hassle') and 'change' trumps 'habit' then 'hassle' must trump 'change'… and if you

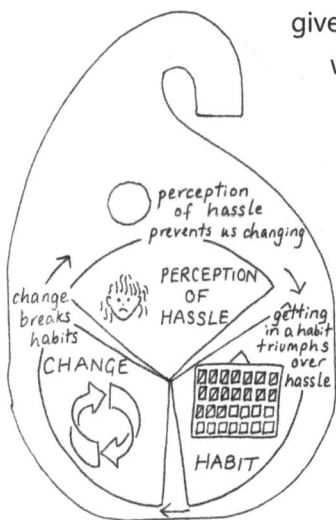

give me a little leeway, you will see it does kind of fit the model.

Habit v. perception of hassle = habit wins

It is possible to overcome my perception of hassle if I get into the habit of doing something.

For example, to begin with it might seem like a huge hassle to get up at 6am and commute for 45 minutes across the county for work, but if I do it every day and get into a routine and make sure I get to bed early the night before, then eventually the habit will overcome the hassle.

Change v. habit = change wins

It is possible for me to overcome a habit if I make a change.

This one is neatly illustrated by how my exercise and healthy eating routines used to get thrown out of the window on holiday, even if I took trainers and running gear and was staying somewhere I could find fruit and yoghurt for breakfast – there was something about the change of scene, the fault-line in my normal patterns of daily life, that threw everything out of kilter.

Hassle v. change = perception of hassle wins

Making a change is made nearly impossible for me, if I *believe* it is going to be a lot of hassle.

I may want to move house, for example, but the thought of all the hassle puts me off – putting the house on the market, preparing it for viewing, selecting estate agents, all the time with legal paperwork, packing, getting removers, informing utilities, and so on and so on.

When it came to writing a novel-sized story and getting it finished, I'd got into bad habits and needed the change of scene and the change of approach to overcome those habits.

A Little Bit About Writing

I was in the local library setting up our local writing group with a writing colleague the other week, when this conversation happened:

Person in library: I couldn't help overhearing: I wrote some poetry and had a book published last year. But I wasn't taught to write or anything.

Me and my writing colleague (in unison): You can't be taught.

You can't be taught to write.

That's what we said.

But we can't have meant that surely?

Everyone knows you can be taught to write: teachers spend plenty of time teaching us to write when we are in primary school – and parents often do at home. Perhaps we learn later, taught by friends or other helpers.

BEING TAUGHT TO WRITE

- We are taught to hold a pen

- We are taught how to shape letters

- We are taught how to construct sentences

Then when we get to secondary school our English teachers tell us how to follow the rules of grammar, they teach us about metaphors and rhymes, about formal and informal language, and so on.

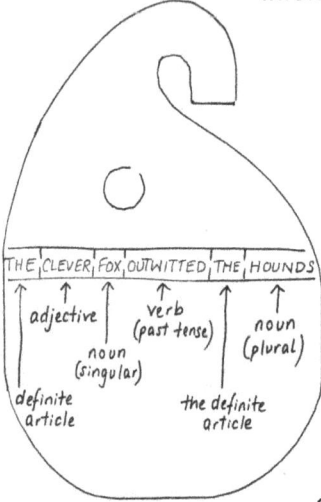

- We are taught correct grammar, spelling, punctuation

THE CLEVER FOX OUTWITTED THE HOUNDS

adjective

verb (past tense)

noun (singular)

noun (plural)

definite article

the definite article

Then there are the many courses on how to write, even degree courses and masters, in creative writing.

We can be taught to write.

We are taught to write.

So what did we mean when we said 'you can't be taught to write'? We must have meant something else.

I don't know what my writing colleague meant but I can begin to tell you what I think I meant.

There must be something that we feel can't be taught. What exactly is it?

I think I meant there is something about communicating successfully that can't be taught, something to which we all have access if we look inside ourselves carefully. There is an essence that gives life to our writing, a magic that enables us to connect with another human being through the use of words. Successful communication through writing is open to us all, because we all have this magic at our fingertips.

You can teach/learn all the rules you want, you can follow all the formulas, you can put all the right ingredients in the mix, but if what you write hasn't got that magic…***that thing that can't be taught***, then it won't work, it won't connect, it won't flow. It won't ring true.

Is it something to do with truth? Honesty? Genuineness? Sincerity? The real-ness of experience?[21] I think so.

It is, maybe, something like a smile. Someone can pull their face into the shape of a smile, they can use all the right muscles and even say nice words to go along with it, but if the smile is not genuine then somehow we know.

a certain smile

And the funny thing is that it's a shapeshifter. This thing that can't be taught. It is difficult to put a finger on. It's not to do with genre. Or style. Or high-brow literature. Writing something that rings true and connects does not belong to an élite band of professional writers penning high-class literary novels. Some writing

---

21 Talking about writing songs, Noel Gallagher on *Desert Island Discs* (BBC Radio 4) said: "There has to be a certain kind of truth in everything you write." (19/07/15)

connects with some people and not with others. Or with some people at some times. Why do I connect with formulaic detective stories when I'm depressed or grieving, for example? I don't know. But I know it works for me. Poetry (most of the time) doesn't work for me – I find poetry a bit too rich, like a tray of honeyed desserts, so I can only consume a very small one once a month or so – but poetry does work for a great many people.

Other people connect with other genres, in different ways at different times.

That's what can't be taught.

How to connect.

And that's why, if we want to write, we must write. Write the truth as we find it. Write honestly. Write

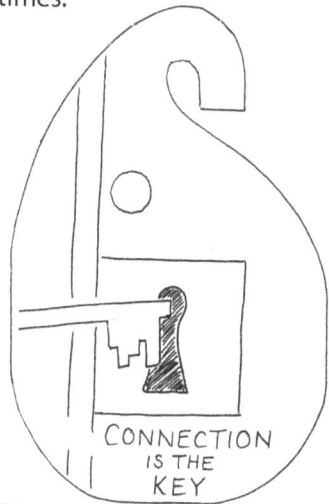

CONNECTION
IS THE
KEY

without fear or favour. Write without wanting a reward. Write for the pleasure of it. Write to connect. Write because, however humble we may feel, what we write may connect with someone at some time.

The fact that it can't be taught (this 'truth', 'connection', 'realness' or whatever the magic is), the fact that it is available to any of us if we look hard enough inside us, doesn't mean it's easy however. It's not easy. Putting words in front of another is easy enough – but making sense is not easy, telling a good story isn't easy, making a connection isn't easy, sticking at it isn't easy. I should know. I've tried and it's darn hard.

Writers' block

I think writers' block is a fallacy. This is connected to my belief that there is no such thing as laziness, just some things that we find more difficult to do at some points. The times when someone could accuse me of laziness are usually times when I am tired...

or possibly times when I am reluctant to move, to get up and get on with a difficult chore. I put off making phone calls because I'm rubbish on the phone, for example, when I can't see someone I find it very difficult to talk to them. So does that make me lazy? I don't think it does. I think it means I find it hard to make phone calls and I need to find ways to make them easier or motivate myself to get them done, or find other ways of communicating. Recognising what I find difficult, and why, is useful information for me; I can work with this information to make myself better, to make life easier, to work to my strengths. If something is holding me back, making me reluctant to move, I need to understand why I am finding it so difficult and take appropriate action to shift the reluctance. Maybe I need to change my mind about something, maybe I need to get in a new habit. I bet you if I made difficult phone calls for a living I'd soon

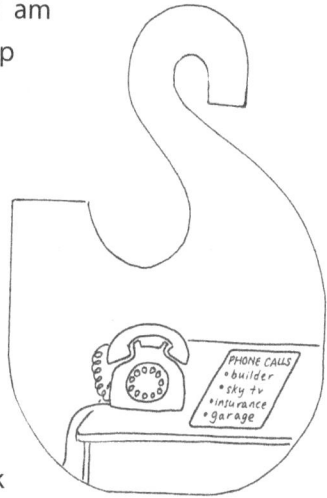

get better at it, even if I never quite overcame my nerves.

So if we think we're suffering from writers' block, what is it exactly that is holding us back? Do we need to shift our mind, our view about something? Do we need to get back in the habit of writing?

I heard an excellent snippet on the radio once, I think, about how artists often think they have to be in the right mood to create, that they have to be touched by the muse. They also said something about the modern world's obsession with motivation and goals (here I must hold my hand up and apologise for having held forth about both these subjects) making people feel they have to feel motivated to get on and do something. But in actual fact, the programme said, we do many things each day that we are not hugely *motivated* to do: for example, we may get up earlier than we want to, we may eat healthily and take exercise, we may visit aged relatives or run our children to football practice, and so on. There are good reasons for doing these things but we are not feeling great motivated desire when we do them – we just get on and do them.

Even if we don't want to work, we can do it.

We don't need to be motivated, we just need to do it.

I've tried doing this and it works.

Because I wrote for pleasure I thought I must *want* to do it to get on and do it. I was sitting there thinking 'oh, that's a pity, I'm not really feeling it today, not in the mood, a whole free morning and I just can't think of anything interesting to write'. If only I had pushed myself to *just do it* I would have pushed past the lack of motivation into the space where the doing it takes over.

The writers' group helps with this.

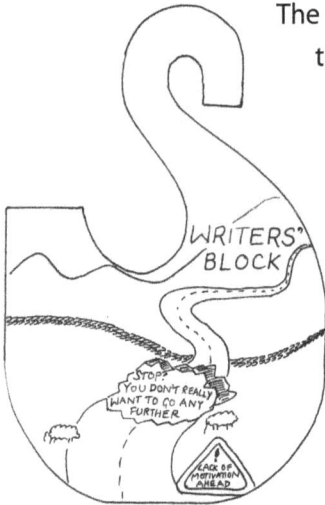

And so did the time pressure of writing a book in a week. I didn't have the space to not feel like writing one morning. I just did it.

So don't worry about not feeling in the mood, do it anyway.

Keep doing it anyway, and the mood will come. Okay, this is as much a reminder to myself as anyone else – I still cannot find my habit of writing every day. But I will.

Learning to write

Okay, so I've mentioned how there may be something about writing that can't be taught, that we have to find by doing, by practising, by trial and error, by writing, and by exploring inside ourselves.

But the fact that this can't be *taught* doesn't mean we can't learn to write.

We just each need to find our own way of learning, of being inspired, motivated and then getting down to it.

I do have several books about writing on my shelves, most of which I have to admit I haven't read, I have just flicked through them. Perhaps I will read them this summer in a bid to write a better novel in a week this autumn.

I have read one book about writing though: Natalie Goldberg's *Wild Mind*.[22]

---

22 *Wild Mind: living the writer's life*, by Natalie Goldberg. 1991, Rider, London.

I read it a long time ago and right now I can't remember much about it except that I absolutely loved it.

Last summer I acquired a set of cassette tapes from a second-hand bookseller which were audiotapes of Natalie Goldberg's other well-known book about writing, *Writing Down the Bones*.[23] I listened to the tapes as I sorted and tidied my workshop one sunny weekend. It was a wonderful and inspiring time. For those hours it was as if Natalie were sitting on the end of the bed settee in my summerhouse talking to me as I tidied up. It is her own voice reading the book on the tapes and she is so natural, it was as if she were in the room with me.

These things I wouldn't hesitate to recommend.

I am sure there are many other extremely good books and resources to help you learn

23   *Writing Down the Bones: freeing the writer within*, by Natalie Goldberg. 1986, Shambhala, Boston, MA.

to write if that's what you want. I'm just mentioning Natalie because she is the person (along with my mum) who has inspired and encouraged me. I also like the fact that she paints, with very vibrant colours.

"there is no excuse. If you want to write, write."

NATALIE GOLDBERG

PART FOUR – DOING IT AGAIN (STARTING TO PLAN THE NEXT BOOK/S)

I first started writing this section in early spring when I had two or three new ideas for stories I wanted to write.

Enthused by the planning process, I was determined to find bigger and better ways to map out the twists in the plot and the interconnections of characters and themes.

At that time, I was also convinced that if I could plan a novel effectively and in detail, I would then be able to write it in addition to my daily life – say, getting up an hour earlier, or setting aside every Sunday afternoon for writing, as some writers do.

Maybe one day I will manage this. But I have to confess that so far this year I have not managed to write (or even start) another novel alongside living my normal busy daily life. (I've been able to write this book over six months, but I find writing non-fiction different, it is easier to do in chunks I've found.)

As I have been writing the other sections of this book, I have been struck by how sweet the six-day-story method is for me. I'm beginning to wonder if I could do it again, perhaps I should try it one more time. Perhaps it is the method for me. Perhaps it will prove to be the only method that works for me. Who knows. I shall experiment and report back.

So the title of this section is another misnomer – I shouldn't really call this section 'doing it again' because I haven't (yet) written another novel, let alone a second book in a week.

But it seemed so apt:

PREPARING→MAKING AND DOING→LEARNING→DOING IT AGAIN

They are the stages I follow when I'm making dresses, or trying my hand at woodwork. It's what I do when I draw an illustration for this book. It's what I do when I'm cooking, or starting a new job, or going on a journey.

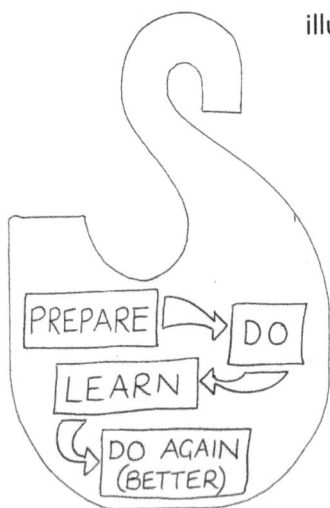

PREPARE → DO

LEARN ←

DO AGAIN (BETTER)

It's the process of inventing and making and learning from our experience – it's what we human beings do.

You can see why I wanted this section to fit the fourth stage of the process. It would be such a good finishing touch.

I can't tell you (yet) what it was like to write another novel in a week.

But I can tell you what it was like to start planning the next story…

Planning The Next Story

I was working with newspaper spread all over the table because it was winter and muddy outside and the cat kept walking muddy footprints onto my table, but then the newspaper came in handy…

A big piece of newspaper folds nicely and it kept all my scruffy ideas in one place.

I thought it's important to me that I use newspaper and rough paper, the back of old bits of paper I was about to throw for recycling, because then it is not too perfect. Perfection is the number one killer of my ideas.

Perfection kills my ideas because it is sterile.

Oh, the perils of perfectionism. Trying to be neat stifles my creativity. I avoid it when I can. Or at least, when I remember.

"want to get things right? use new perfection"

kills all creativity

100% Sterile

KILLS 100% OF NEW IDEAS

PERFECTION

Also, if what I'm working on is scruffy it really doesn't matter if I change something – I can always stick something over it and start again. It doesn't matter if the cat walks muddy footprints all over my work, it doesn't matter if I put my mug of tea down on it and it leaves a mark, it doesn't matter if it gets torn, I can just paste another scrap of paper over it and/or work round it.

I tried to keep things scruffy, knowing that otherwise I would want to do a neat version too soon, I would want to make it look nice, but I know the sketching stage isn't finished yet. It's the same when I'm drawing, I have to keep things rough and a bit scruffy while I'm working on them, and then neaten them up when I know I'm on the right track.

I found I was looking at what was left on the newspaper and the torn scraps of paper I was using and found it inspired me and sometimes linked to things I hadn't thought of before. Like doodling and brainstorming can free up areas of our minds; like yoga used muscles I didn't even know I had.

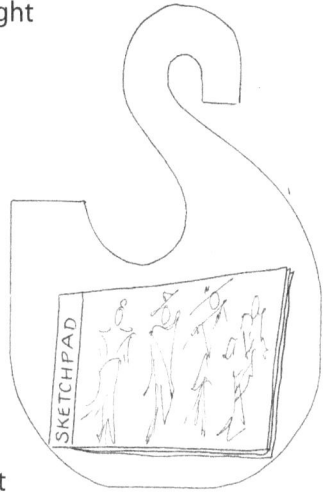

All is good, all is valid, nothing is thrown out at this stage. Everything and anything can be useful. This is a time for great flexibility of mind. Will I use this or will I consider that?

I made the first newspaper spread deliberately messy so I felt I could scribble all over it and add bits and it won't mess it up because it's already messy. I thought to myself that I could always make a neat version when I've decided (more or less) how things were going to look. At this stage I needed flexibility.

I discovered I was pasting up bits of paper that had charts on that I used to use for monitoring what I ate – this was interesting to me because since I have been focussing on writing and making things I now get so involved in what I am writing or making that I don't fret about what I eat any more, I don't overeat, I don't worry about what I look like and my weight has found a natural balance. Basically I am way more interested in my ideas and finding a way to design, write or make them. They are a focus outside of myself, beyond the petty stressy controlling thoughts of my ego, beyond my self-absorbed mind. This reminds me of something I learnt about addiction, obsession, and overthinking (when I was probably doing all of those things) – focussing on activities based outside of ourselves, concentrating on actions of value to others and to the community, these things form part of the journey back to healthy functioning and away from addictive and obsessive behaviour.

Or maybe the controlling calories, monitoring what I ate, learning about nutrition, what was good for me, what worked and what didn't, was part of the process I had to go through to get to where I am now. Like the other ups and downs. Like the therapy, the friendships, the training courses, the past relationships, all the many and varied learning experiences that add up to the happy place I'm now at. Perhaps it all had to be assimilated, taken in and filtered

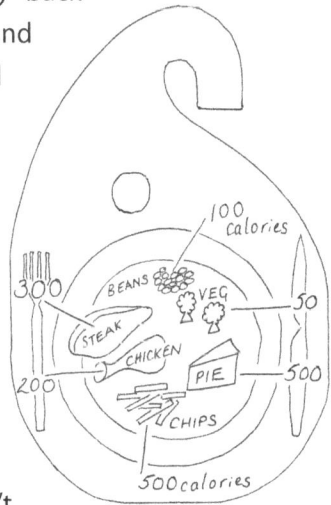

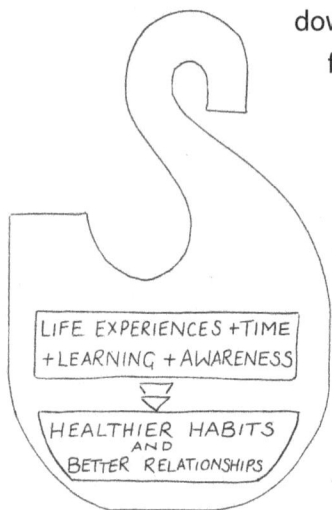

down, so that I could learn, form new and healthier habits.

LIFE EXPERIENCES + TIME + LEARNING + AWARENESS

HEALTHIER HABITS AND BETTER RELATIONSHIPS

When I was making this first spread of ideas on newspaper, I found I was also pasting up paper where the back had print-outs of Ten Top Tips to Transform Your Relationship. This was interesting to me because I am so much happier alone now than I used to be in relationships. This says something about the quality, depth, and dynamics of the relationships I have had in the past ten years. But it also says something about me. Writing, designing, making, all these things more than adequately fill the space where a relationship used to be. Which came first? Did I want to write and design and make and so I needed to lose the emotional clutter of complicated, needy, interdependent romantic relationships to make space to do the creative things I longed to do? Or did I miraculously find that, once I was free of troublesome romance and desire, I had all this wonderful peace and me-space that allowed me to work on things that I found so much more rewarding? Perhaps it just worked in tandem, synchronised. Something about life timing, serendipity: when things fall into place.

As I jotted down some notes about a couple of scenes I'd imagined while swimming the day before, I noticed how each jotting filled a similar amount of space, a bit rectangular post-it sized I suppose, but I didn't have any post-its to hand, I had a lot of scrap paper and I was thinking how freeing it was to use scraps in this way, it meant that nothing felt fixed, everything could shift with my thoughts and ideas and the way the characters revealed parts of the story to me.

On some of the paper I was tearing up were some things we'd previously used the paper for – there were the words 'petrol' and 'bread', clearly the beginnings of a shopping list but I decided to leave them on the paper and see where they went as ideas, maybe petrol and bread could feature in part of the story. I like things introducing themselves without me controlling everything – welcome the random I say.

On another piece of paper there was an elephant, which reminds me to remind you about chunking again – how do you eat an elephant? Not all in one go of course. In small mouthfuls, bit by bit. Not that I would recommend eating an elephant, they are wonderful creatures that demand respect and need protection from poachers, however I am sure you understand the image. If you want to take on a big task, it is important to break it down into small parts in order to make it manageable. And writing a book is a mammoth task, right? The thought of it had certainly overwhelmed me before now.

So back to the tearing up of paper.

If you take an A4 sheet and tear it in half and then tear the halves in half and then tear the quarters in half, you will have 8 more-or-less equally sized scraps where there is enough room to write down the brief description of a scene-event.

I did this with 4 sheets of A4, so I had a paper-patch for each one of my 32 scene-events.

I wrote out 32 scene-events (happenings) onto my scraps of paper.

Then I played about with them, rearranged them, shuffled them, pinned them up onto a pinboard – to see how the ideas fitted together and to try to develop a plot.

After a while I realised I'd run out of ideas for the day. Don't get down about it, I said to myself, just pop your ideas away and get on with something completely different for a while. Just come back to it when you have more ideas.

You see how this book contains instructions to me.

When I was roughing out ideas for the people in the second book, I noticed I was calling them by their initials again, as I did for the first book. I remembered how difficult it was to stop myself thinking of them as A, B and C when I was writing the first book because I'd been thinking of them in my head as A, B and C all the time that I'd been imagining them in their scenes and they had been talking to me about their lives. I vowed to name the people in the second book swiftly and fully, so that when I thought of them and they talked to me I would know them by their names and it would then be so much easier to write them as their full names when I wrote the second book.

When roughing out ideas for another, and different, book, I realised I would have to prevent myself from starting to write until I had a plan complete. This was because I knew that, if I let the writing start, the writing would take over and go off on its own tangent. That is one of the things that had happened before when I'd started stories without a full plot mapped out. I do believe some (proper) writers set off writing without a plan but I also know what I'm like and I know the only way I'll have a coherent (this is important) narrative is if I stick to the plan.

Holding myself back from writing when I wanted to write was like holding a greyhound in the traps, keeping a rodeo bull in the pen snorting at the gate to be freed. If only I could bottle the energy for the moment when I had time to start...

READY TO GO

The Importance of Coherence

I used to be an editor. Not a big shot editor dealing with internationally renowned authors; just a common-or-garden everyday copy-editor – someone who reads through a book before it is published to check the spelling, punctuation, grammar, accuracy, consistency, writing style and so on. I was reasonably good at it at the time – probably because I was still a perfectionist then.

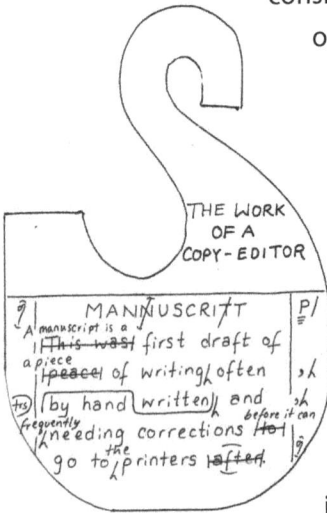

THE WORK
OF A
COPY-EDITOR

MANUSCRIPT
A manuscript is a
This was first draft of
a piece of writing often
written by hand and
frequently needing corrections before it can
go to the printers after

One of the things I find jumps out at me when I read books (as well as the typos) is a lack of consistency. Yes, it's irritating (to me) and noticeable (to me) when a book spells a person's name in two different ways – in the chapter of the book I read last night, the same woman was referred to as Mrs Daniel and Mrs Daniels, I found myself checking back to see which one was the right one. But worse than this is a lack of consistency to do with the place or the people or the theme of the book. And that's because a lack of consistency leads to a book lacking coherence.

Just as a typo makes the reader falter, hesitate, re-read a section, equally a lack of consistency in character (unless it is deliberate) or in place or theme will add jolts and jumps to the narrative that will threaten to make our stories fall apart. At best, we may look unprofessional, at worst it could make our story thoroughly confusing and unreadable.

Take, for example, one of the first scenes of an action film where an important character walks into a meeting with her handbag. She places it on the floor by her chair, in one shot we can see it by the chair, in the next shot it is no longer there. The character walks out of the room without the bag. For someone like me, this is very disconcerting. I spent the next few minutes wondering if this were deliberate – was there something in the bag and she had left it there intentionally?

Were we to assume that someone had taken her bag? As there is no further reference to her handbag I ended up assuming it was a mistake, but it confused me...and stopped the flow of the film. If I'd been at home watching it on the dvd player, I would have paused and rewound to see what happened to the bag.

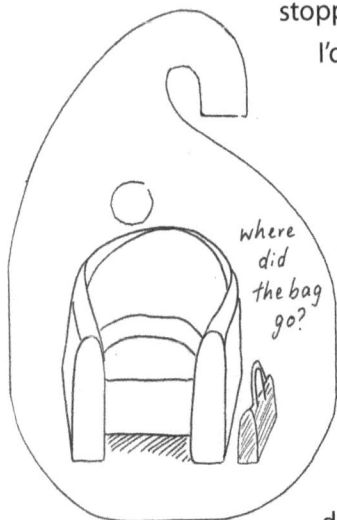

where did the bag go?

Continuity checkers. Those are the people that check those things on film aren't they? I definitely need them. I knew there were things I missed while I was planning, and plotting and writing the story I wrote in a week, so I welcomed my family reading my first draft and telling me when they didn't understand why someone had said that thing or what had happened to the note left on the sink and why didn't she know where he had got to that night, and so on. It's sometimes much easier for a fresh eye to spot those inconsistencies.

Coherence in a story is important because our minds will reject incoherence – even if the incoherent is the truth. How often I have found myself assuming something about a phrase or a sentence or a situation or a relationship that I overhear or observe round me just because it *made sense*. I'm pretty certain we are built to make sense out of situations, even where there is no sense; similarly to how we are designed to make purpose. So, when it comes to story-telling, coherence is key. Have you ever found yourself not believing in a character on tv or in a play? Have you ever found yourself saying: "but they just wouldn't have said something like that!" or thought a plot didn't ring true? That's a lack of coherence – it didn't fit. It didn't fit with the way our minds wanted to make sense of it. Similarly, in stories (films, books, plays) we can get away with all sorts of extreme events if they are coherent within the world we have created.

"but they just wouldn't have said something like that!"

Our minds love coherence. This explains to me why I (and others) have been so upset in the past when something incoherent, incomprehensible has happened, if someone has acted out of character, if something has happened at the wrong time, an untimely death, a stable person breaking down, a dependable person leaving – it just doesn't fit.

I can do nothing about the past. I can learn from the past to inform my decisions in the future. I can take more care, become more observant, look after myself and others, make sure I am thoughtful – and keep my mind accepting of a world of possibilities. The incoherent may happen, but it may feel less incomprehensible, less difficult to accept, if I keep an open mind.

Thankfully, when it comes to stories, we can check for coherence as we go along. I can check and double check my 30-step plans and my ideas for plots. I can test my writing in my writing group. I can take my stories to be read by long-suffering friends and family, and even by editors and agents perhaps.

And if I want to introduce crazy wild events into a book, I may just be able to do this… as long as it feels believable in the context, as long as the story is coherent.

Life, as they say, can be stranger than fiction. Because we make fiction up, there is always the risk that the reader may shout at us: "I don't believe you! You're making all this up!" There's more pressure on the writer to be believable than there is on life.

Notes to Self

I have often said to my children (they are probably tired of hearing it) that we learn more from losing than we do from winning. This used to be when I was trying to cheer up one of them after they had lost a match, but it can hold true for many areas of our lives. We can learn more from things that are

PREPARING → DOING → LEARNING → DOING AGAIN

PREPARE DO

REVIEW

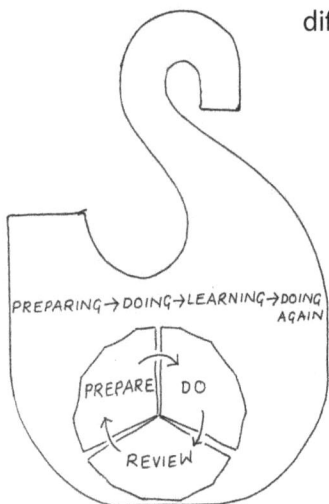

difficult than from things we find easy: I imagine that the emotions we go through when we are suffering or struggling sort of imprint a message deeper into our minds, so that we can learn more from it if we analyse the experience well. Maybe something like that. While editing this book this summer, I heard a radio programme where schoolchildren were inspired to take on more difficult challenges because they had learnt that their brain would grow from trial and error, from struggling with difficult problems.[24] I read somewhere once that it took Eddison 279 attempts to make a light bulb that worked. The final attempt worked. The previous 278 attempts weren't failures – they were *trials*, he said. I also read (possibly somewhere else) that human beings are natural scientists – we experiment. That makes sense to me. It seems to me that we are

24   BBC Radio 4, *Carol Dweck and Growth Mindset*, on Mind Changers with Claudia Hammond, 12/08/15.

designed to learn, that feels like our purpose. And to complete the cycle it feels natural to me that I would want to give the novel-in-a-week a second go – can I do it again? Was it a one-hit wonder, just a fluke or can I repeat the process and achieve it again? More importantly, can I do it again and do it better?

IT TOOK 279 ATTEMPTS TO MAKE A LIGHT BULB THAT WORKED (APPARENTLY)

If I am to give the novel-in-a-week another go, and if I'm to do it as well if not better, then I will need to have learnt from what I experienced. What have I learnt about the difficulties and problems of writing a book in six days and what can I do differently next time?

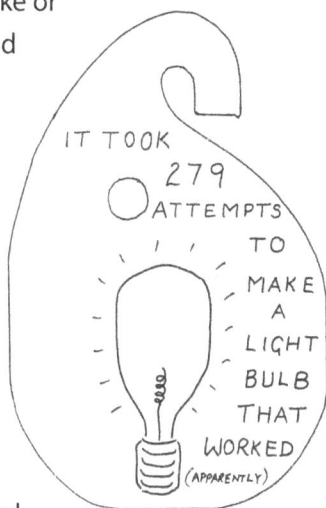

When I looked back on the story I wrote in a week, I found it really difficult to pick out the mentions of time and location. I was attempting to shift the timeline slightly, and I also wanted to check the locations fitted the rough map I had in my head, but it was really difficult to do in reverse. With the next story, I am going to sketch out timelines, and make a rough map as I do the planning and the writing – so I know where I am. However, I still think that altering the times or the locations would be very difficult after the story is written, so I need to get this right at the planning stage.

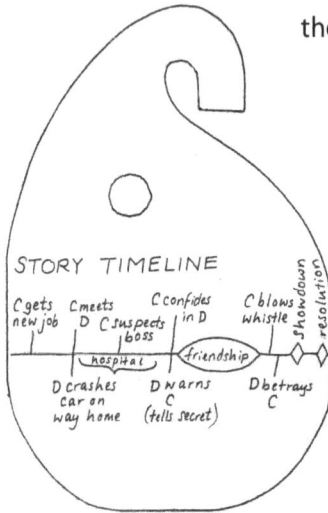

STORY TIMELINE

C gets new job

C meets D

C confides in D

C blows whistle

C suspects boss

showdown

resolution

hospital

friendship

D crashes car on way home

D warns C (tells secret)

D betrays C

Then there's the naming of people – I won't be calling them all A, B, C, D, and E in the plan for the next story, that's for sure.

What other 'notes to self' are there?

More planning I think.

If I have learnt anything about writing a novel in a week, then it is the importance of planning as much as possible in advance.

And more practice.

If I want my writing 'style' to be better – less clichéd, more thoughtful, less waffly, more snappy – if I want my characters to be more round and whole and engaging, if I want my threads and themes to be more involving and at the same time truthful in a truth-about-human-nature way, then I will need to practise, practise, practise.

"Practise your scales every day"

Whether I write 60,000 words in six days or six months, whether I am running a marathon or a sprint, I need to practise to run the kind of race I want to run. The sort of ease I see in artists and performers and sports people is achieved after years of practice. Perhaps I shall set myself a routine, a writing routine of practice exercises that I shall do on a regular basis – like the 30 minutes of piano practice I was supposed to do as a child: scales and arpeggios, then running through my current repertoire.

As Natalie Goldberg (and others) have said: if you want to be a writer, then write.

And I have said similarly to my children, if you want to get good at something then practise. I remember one of my sons being irritated that he wasn't good at tennis – it was perhaps the second time he had ever picked up a tennis raquet, being naturally adept at most sports he had thought he'd be able to play tennis almost instantly. In fact, it didn't take him long to learn – but he did have to accept there would be a short period of learning and practising before he could return the ball across the net and score points against his brother.

So it is with writing.

I have picked up the raquet. This doesn't mean I can play tennis yet.

Practice is…training for the moments under pressure when you have to go into autopilot, the moment when paramedics say 'the training just kicked in'.

With this as my metaphor, then if I practise writing until my writing style becomes second nature, then when I am under time pressure my training should kick in and I should (in theory) write in the style I want even when I don't have time to think about it.

By trying to write I have learnt some of the things I can do and some of the things

I struggle with, I have learnt a good deal about myself and about how I see the world – perhaps I have learnt some things about being human too, or at least about my own version of being human.

In order to learn more and to get better (at writing and at being human), I need to keep trying, I need to give it another go.

Trying Again

I'm nervous of trying again.

I wonder if it won't be as good an experience. What if my second novel is worse? What if I don't get it finished in a week?

But if I don't try then I'll always wonder – was my achievement of writing a novel in less than a week just beginners' luck?

They say, apparently, that we regret the things we don't do more than the things we do. Susan Jeffers[25] says we should 'feel the fear and do it anyway'. I thank her for this – the quote and the book, I came across both a while back, at just the right stage of my life, and they seem particularly apt now.

It is scary to write a book and put it out there – to be read or rejected. I have to be brave.

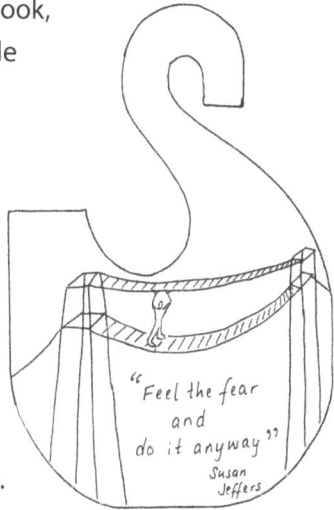

"Feel the fear and do it anyway"
Susan Jeffers

I may not go away to write for a week this year, and, if I don't, perhaps I will find it hard to complete a story without my completion zone – my writing convent.

One of the things that haunts me particularly is the thought that I may be able to write

25 *Feel the Fear and Do It Anyway*, by Susan Jeffers. 2007, Vermilion, London

but perhaps I am not (yet?) able to write well. Perhaps I won't connect with people. And if I try to write another novel in a week perhaps this won't help me learn to write well. Will it be just another race against time? Will it be just another exercise in focus and completion? Will it be just another way of proving myself, trying to show someone I can get things done? A stroppy rebel shouting; rushed and powerful rather than cultivated and nurtured.

I wonder: is it possible to harness the focus and energy, the fluidity and coherence I achieved when writing a story in a week and yet to *choose* words and to write with thought and consideration?

My feeling now is that this may be possible – but it may not be possible for me straight away.

It may be that for some time for me writing under time pressure will produce one kind of novel (energetic, coherent, together) – and a finished one – and writing without time pressure may be the arena where I develop my own style and can practise forming character and dialogue, a view and a voice.

I may just have to accept that this second route ends up with a small pile of unfinished novels, short stories and exercises, while my writing weeks away are where I prove to myself that I can finish things.

CONCLUSION

Choice

'There is no right and no wrong, only choices.'
So said my counsellor ten years ago.

This statement is, of course, debateable and subject to the circumstances in which it is uttered.

At the time I was probably insisting that there was a 'right' way to do things and that I felt I had failed because I hadn't got things 'right'. I can't remember exactly but that was a theme of much of my therapy at the time.

I did, however, find the bold 'no right and no wrong' statement invigorating, liberating. It challenged all the cultural conditioning I had taken in over the previous forty years.

As a result of the following ten years of exploration and experimentation, I would add to the phrase:

There is no right and wrong

Only choices

And each choice has consequences.

Imagine a path through the woods. You are surrounded by trees and cannot see the landscape outside the forest. You don't know where the rivers are, where the towns are, where the dangerous precipice is, or where the friendly villagers will be. In fact you don't know if any of these things exist or not, and you are not entirely clear where you are going, what you are aiming for, what you want or what is possible. You have a vague sense that almost anything is possible, that some things you meet may be more difficult to experience than other things. You also know that you will be more able to cope well in some situations than others, but you are not sure what those situations are until you meet them.

When you come to a clearing, there are several routes outwards, all leading further into the forest ...and possibly to worlds beyond the forest, you can sense they are out there somewhere. But which route to take? And will you measure up to what you find on the path?

"there is no right or wrong ~ there are only choices"

CHOICE CHOICE
CONSEQUENCES
CONSEQUENCES
STOP

There is no right or wrong path, only the choice you make and the consequences that follow from that choice.

I live in the north-west of Britain. Not the high north-west, with the dramatic Lakeland mountains and the poetic daffodil-strewn fells. I live in the warm, wet area between Manchester and Liverpool and Preston. As an incomer, I have been warmly welcomed by Lancastrians. As a northern convert, I love my adopted region with a fierceness I never felt about the north-of-London commuter-belt I grew up in. But it is rainy land. Umbrellas and wellies are staples, particularly when you live, as we do, down an un-made-up track with puddles front and back. My mother delights in sending me texts about the weather in the south-east: 'so sunny here darling, the lawn is parched', 'what a glorious week of summer we've had' she texts, as the storms rumble over the fields at the back of our house, all the heat turning into clouds over the Pennines and showering unseasonal hailstones into our back yard. Sixteen years living in Leeds taught me to wrap up against a biting wind and winters brought proper snow again. Sixteen years on the other side of the Pennines has taught me that it may always rain…at almost any time…but that it will also blow over. We sometimes have delightfully fresh, clear, sunny evenings when the winds from the coast 20 minutes away blow the clouds back onto the Pennines. Through the weather I have learnt (the hard way) that, just as there is no right or wrong, there is also no good and bad: there is no good or bad weather,

"there's no such thing as bad weather, just the wrong clothes"

there is just the wrong clothes for the type of weather we're in.

So if there is no right or wrong, and no good or bad, then what conclusions can I draw from my experience of writing a novel in a week and thinking about what I've learnt from it?

There's no right or wrong way to write or to get things done, just what works for you at the time…is that what I can say?

What about good and bad? Is there good and bad writing? If my goal is to communicate and I achieve that, then on some level that must be 'good' or at least okay. If my goal is to communicate with a certain audience and I don't achieve that, because I use the wrong language for them or because I don't engage them, or I fail to empathise, then, however beautiful my prose, nevertheless my writing isn't good enough.

It depends on the goal. And on what we are using to measure 'achievement' of the goal.

Things are only as good or bad, right or wrong, as the frame of measurement we impose from the outside. If there is no measurement, then the concepts of success and failure, good and bad, right and wrong can't exist.

I set my goal and I achieved it.

I can conclude that my personal experiment was a success.

GOOD = GOAL = SUCCESS

Adequate	Nearly there
Getting better	On the way
Not good enough yet	Keep trying
	Just starting out

You may set different personal goals and achieve different results.

It's all terribly, wonderfully individual.

Making the Point

Despite fighting valiantly to say that I can only speak for me, to beware of generalisations, I can't stop myself wanting to draw general conclusions from my experience.

Studying psychology frustrated me: for every six studies that proved that young children benefitted from attending nursery, there were another half a dozen that proved young children benefitted from being cared for at home by a family member. (At the time my youngest son was four years old and I worked from home.) It appeared as if no over-riding conclusions could be drawn about the 'best' way to bring up children. This made sense. There are as many 'good' ways to bring up children as there are combinations of children and parents – we are all so individual, and what works for one of us may not work for another. And yet some general conclusions can be drawn out of all the specifics – as long as we include the provisos...

So I can say with confidence that what worked for me *may* work for someone else, because despite all our individuality, we human beings are built of similar stuff – we can experience joy and pain, love and fear, we have a range of movement and abilities, we know what it is to be human.

MANY GOOD WAYS TO BRING UP CHILDREN

And it is the possibility that it *may* work for someone else too that entices me to share my experience.

I see people as makers and do-ers.

We live in an internal world mapped out in our heads, coloured by our feelings; nevertheless in the outside world of other people, society and culture, we are defined

by our actions – by the things we make, do and say.

Seeing people as makers means I also see people as learners.

PREPARING → MAKING AND DOING → LEARNING → DOING IT AGAIN

We are creators (idea) and inventors (plan/ design) and craftspeople (make).

A   →   B   →   C

IDEA   →   PLAN   →   ACTION

And, for me, the process of idea-plan-action is quintessentially human, it is one of the things we are designed, have developed (as creatures), to do

...and this process gives us a sense of purpose

...and we learn from it.

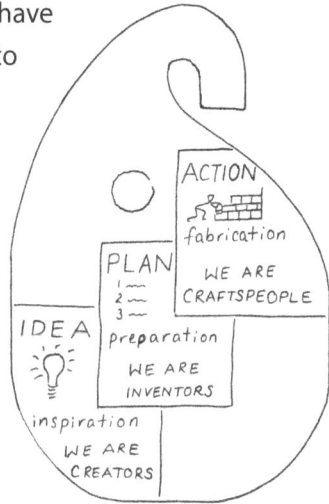

When we have learnt from the process, we can then improve our skills for the next time we go through the process and it seems natural that we want to share our learning with those we care about and the rest of the world.

This is why I want to write.

And, now I reflect on it, this is why I've written this book.

I thought I was writing a book about completion, but in fact I have possibly been writing a book about learning from experience and sharing that experience.

Who Have I Written This Book For?

If someone had asked me who I wanted to write this book for, I would have said I was writing it for my children. But when I think of the examples I've mentioned (in this book and at other times), then I remember how very wise my children are and how little they need a book from me.

Right from the time they were tiny and started expressing themselves, I have felt I was learning easily as much from my children as they might learn from me. So often they have said things that have astounded me with their wisdom, it was as if they were born knowing things that I have had to find out the hard way, as if they were in touch with a source of innate in-built information about the world and about people that I have only recently begun to understand, appreciate and incorporate into my life.

I do wonder if they are all three naturally more emotionally intelligent than me. Remember that stuff I said earlier about how I tend to intellectualise things? My mind tends to analyse and abstract ideas, and my children appear to be more connected with their internal emotional world than I have been until now.

Also for some of the last ten years I have been wrapped up in my own issues and unable to see past my own emotional clutter to get a different perspective. When I was too busy or self-absorbed to see, my children were able to point out things to me that were glaringly obvious from the outside. Like the time when I was moaning about how I wanted to be loved for the person I was inside rather than how I looked, and my youngest suggested, if this were what I really wanted, then I should spend less time on my hair and make-up. I love how frank my children can be with me.

So I know I don't need to write this book for my children. They know it all already. Or if they don't know it all yet, then they are well equipped to enjoy learning it all in their own way.

In fact, I firmly believe that there are many things we all already know...but have somehow lost sight of in the business of our lives.

Sometimes, during therapy, when I had a penny-dropping moment, when I realised something about myself, one of those 'aha!' moments when suddenly the confusion slips away like mist and I could see the way things were like a landscape laid out before me, sometimes then it seemed as if I had always known this piece of truth but it had just been hidden from me. Hidden from me by something I was doing or believing. Hidden from me by some sort of defensive refusal to see the truth, a thick hedge I had grown up inside my head to stop myself feeling bad about something.

Yoga philosophy talks about 'avidja' – how our vision of how things really are in the world and with ourselves can be obscured by a kind of cloud of confusion, a smokescreen of mistaken beliefs. A bit like a fog of prejudice that has to be swept away by a direct experience of reality, or a dark night on a rocky coastline that has to be lit up by a lighthouse.

We know it all already.

Sometimes we simply need a little help to see (feel) clearly what we already know.

When I was working in the prison, running thinking skills workshops for offenders, those on the group would often stop us and say: 'but we know all this already. We know it is wiser to stop and think. We know to count to ten and breathe deeply before we rush in. We know it makes sense to weigh up the pros and cons before we make a decision.' And I would say 'I know you know this, but do you use these skills every day? Do you put it into action?'

I need reminders.

I have a strong suspicion I have written this book for myself; it may be one long list of 'notes to self'.

APPENDIX I

MY RECIPE CARD FOR WRITING A BOOK IN A WEEK

Essential ingredients:

1. **FAITH –** Belief in my ability

2. **LOVE –** Wanting to have a go

3. **SPACE –** Safe space to relax and be inventive

4. **SUPPORT –** Someone who understands and gives the right kind of support

5. **SHARING –** An audience, whether they give feedback or not

6. **EFFORT –** Being content to give up pleasures and put in the hard work

Additional ingredients:

Focus – I excluded distractions, and pared life down to a minimum – all my energy was focussed in one direction.

Commitment – and accountability – I had a personal contract with myself and tied my supporters into this.

Provision – I had comfort and encouragement – I had Maslow's hierarchy of needs well covered.

Preparation – I had done my planning; I had my route map, and now could concentrate on 'painting by numbers'.

Practice – I had carried out my tests, I knew I could do it; I had some basic writing experience – this gave me both realism and confidence.

Method:

1.   Use knowledge and motivation

I knew what I was doing and I wanted to do it very much.

2.   Follow this route:

Define your goal → visualise the benefits → be specific about the details → keep your vision in mind → while you take steps towards your goal

3.   Mix with momentum

Utensils:

•   Plan a timetable and stick to it

•   Use time restriction as a focussing tool

APPENDIX II

YOUR RECIPE CARD FOR WRITING A BOOK IN A WEEK

INGREDIENTS

-
-
-
-

METHOD

-
-
-
-

AFTER WORDS

Oliver Burkeman on obligation versus autonomy:

'Anything […] can be made dispiriting by being turned into an obligation. This is why you should think carefully before following the popular path of turning your "passion" – reupholstering antique chairs, say – into a career. Once you've absolutely got to do it, at 9am on a rainy Thursday, you could find yourself worse off than before: stuck with a job you can't stand, only now without the benefits of an escapist hobby at weekends.'

The Guardian, 17/07/15

Dianne Doubtfire on plotting a novel:

Dianne was in conversation with Winston Clewes, she explained:

"'I want to start a novel," I said, "but it's all just a muddle in my mind. How can I sort it out?"

His answer was invaluable. He advised me to write the numbers 1–30 down the left-hand side of a sheet of foolscap paper and against number 1 to jot down a note about a possible opening. Against number 30, one could write an idea for an ending, and against various other numbers (perhaps only a few at first) brief notes on some highspots in the story.'

The Craft of Novel-Writing, by Dianne Doubtfire. 1987, Allison & Busby, London. Page 11.

An Addition to the Motivation Equation:

When discussing the motivation equation with my son, we decided there was a third factor to take into account, not just where we are now (A) and where we are going (B). This third factor is how we get there. We called this P for process, for the process of getting from A to B.

It is important to remember that we are dealing with our perceptions as much as, if not more than, reality, because our decisions will be based on our emotions however much logic we try to throw at them.

So in order to motivate ourselves to go from A (where we feel we are now) to B (some future situation), P (the process of getting there) needs to appear at least do-able and not too overwhelmingly costly in terms of time, money and emotional energy. The best possible option is if P appears enjoyable.

We may, for example, feel we are unfit and we would like to become fit. If the process of becoming fit looks fun and enjoyable, if we love the idea of regular dance classes or joining a rambling group, then that will look like a net gain to us – we love the process and we want the end goal.

On the other hand, it may be we don't mind our current job but we are being made redundant and will need to get another job. If the process of applying for jobs and going for job interviews feels like a huge effort, then we will need to find a job we really like the look of to motivate ourselves to go through that process.

Here is how the motivation equation works with the process added to it.

A is our perception of where we're at now

B is our perception of some future situation

P is our perception of the process of getting from A to B

All of these are measured in units of difficulty or 'unpleasant effort'.

In order to motivate ourselves to go from A to B:

A needs to appear less good than B – it seems more of an unpleasant effort to remain at A than to be at B.

B needs to appear better than A – it seems less of an unpleasant effort to be at B than to be at A.

P needs to appear at least do-able and possibly even pleasant and, we hope, enjoyable even if effortful – the amount of unpleasant effort required to move from A to B is less than the amount of unpleasant effort required for staying at A.

Measured in units of unpleasant effort,

$$A > B + P = M$$
$$(M = \text{motivation to move}).$$

A needs to feel more unpleasant than B and P combined in order for us to be motivated to move from A to B.

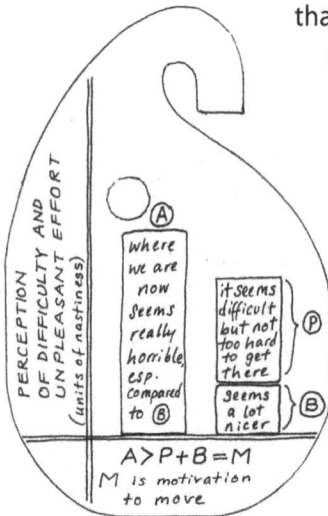

PERCEPTION OF DIFFICULTY AND UNPLEASANT EFFORT (units of nastiness)

(A) where we are now seems really horrible, esp. compared to (B)

it seems difficult but not too hard to get there (P)

seems a lot nicer (B)

A>P+B=M
M is motivation to move

The great news is that we can change our perceptions about all three of these elements by feeding information into our thoughts.

REFERENCES AND RESOURCES

A list of books and resources you might find interesting, some of which I've mentioned in the text.

I did no specific research for this book – I only looked inside my own mind, however I have read an awful lot of really good books in my life and many of them were around me while I wrote this.

Internet sources were accessed in August 2015.

References

http://www.theguardian.com/lifeandstyle/2015/jul/17/more-sex-please-but-just-dont-tell-us-to-do-it – for Oliver Burkeman on obligation versus autonomy.

http://www.forensicsolutions.co.uk/SE3R.htm –
for Dr Eric Shepherd and the SE3R storyboard.

http://www.belbin.com/content/page/49/
BELBIN(uk)-2011-TeamRoleSummaryDescriptions.
pdf) – for team role descriptions.

A Room of One's Own, by Virginia Woolf. 1945,
Penguin, London.

The Craft of Novel-Writing, by Dianne Doubtfire.
1987, Allison & Busby, London.

https://en.wikipedia.org/wiki/
Yerkes%E2%80%93Dodson_law – for more on
the performance-arousal curve.

The House at Pooh Corner, by A. A. Milne. 1928,
Methuen, London. Illustration by E. H. Shepherd.
With thanks to google images.

Motivation and Personality, by Abraham H.
Maslow. 1954, Harper, NY.

https://en.wikipedia.org/wiki/Maslow%27s_
hierarchy_of_needs – for Maslow's hierarchy of
needs with illustrations.

Scarcity: why having too little means so much,
by Sendhil Mullainathan and Eldar Shafir. 2013,
Allen Lane, London.

Thinking, Fast and Slow, by Daniel Kahneman.
2011, Penguin, London.

http://www.bbc.co.uk/programmes/b062hplj –
for Noel Gallagher on BBC Radio 4's *Desert Island
Discs.*

Wild Mind: living the writer's life, by Natalie Goldberg. 1991, Rider, London.

Writing Down the Bones: freeing the writer within, by Natalie Goldberg. 1986, Shambhala, Boston, MA.

http://www.bbc.co.uk/programmes/b062jsn7 – for BBC Radio 4's programme on Carol Dweck and the growth mindset.

Feel the Fear and Do It Anyway, by Susan Jeffers. 2007, Vermilion, London.

Please note: I have not necessarily read all the way through all of these books, some of them I have just dipped into from time to time, and some are on my shelves waiting to be read properly.

There are also many more that I will have forgotten to mention – this is just a list of those most immediately to hand. See it perhaps as a starting point, a taster, a few suggestions for further reading, if you want. If you are interested in the same things as me, of course, you may have read all these, and more, already.

Writing

The Seven Basic Plots: why we tell stories, by Christopher Booker. 2004, Continuum, London.

Becoming a Writer, by Dorothea Brande. 1983, Papermac, London.

The Craft of Novel-Writing, by Dianne Doubtfire. 1987, Allison & Busby, London.

Wild Mind: living the writer's life, by Natalie Goldberg. 1991, Rider, London.

Writing Down the Bones: freeing the writer within, by Natalie Goldberg. 1986, Shambhala, Boston, MA.

Writing the Natural Way: using right-brain techniques to release your expressive powers, by Gabriele Lusser Rico. 1983, Jeremy P. Tarcher Inc., CA.

Why I Write, by George Orwell. 2004, Penguin, London.

Fowler's Modern English Usage. 1983, OUP, Oxford.

Hart's Rules for Compositors and Readers. 1983, OUP, Oxford.

New Oxford Dictionary for Writers and Editors. 2005, OUP, Oxford.

A Room of One's Own, by Virginia Woolf. 1945, Penguin, London.

Learning about Ourselves

Weekend Life Coach: how to get the life you want in 48 hours, by Lynda Field. 2004, Vermilion, London.

Build Your Own Rainbow: a workbook for career and life management, by Barrie Hopson and Mike Scally. 1984, Lifeskills Associates, Leeds.

Feel the Fear and Do It Anyway, by Susan Jeffers. 2007, Vermilion, London.

Embracing Uncertainty: achieving peace of mind as we face the unknown, by Susan Jeffers. 2003, Hodder and Stoughton, London.

How to be Confident Using the Power of NLP, by David Molden and Pat Hutchinson. 2008, Pearson Education Ltd, Harlow.

I Could Do Anything If I Only Knew What It Was: how to discover what you really want and how to get it, by Barbara Sher with Barbara Smith. !994, Delacorte Press, NY.

It's Only Too Late If You Don't Start Now: how to create your second life after 40, by Barbara Sher. 1998, Delacorte Press, NY.

Live the Life You Love, in ten easy step-by-step lessons, by Barbara Sher. 1996, Delacorte Press, NY.

Learning about the World and People

Quiet: the power of introverts in a world that can't stop talking, by Susan Cain. 2012, Viking, London.

Affluenza: how to be successful and stay sane, by Oliver James. 2007, Vermilion, London.

Thinking, Fast and Slow, by Daniel Kahneman. 2011, Penguin, London.

Scarcity: why having too little means so much, by Sendhil Mullainathan and Eldar Shafir. 2013, Allen Lane, London.

Happiness

True Happiness: your complete guide to emotional health, by Dr Mark Atkinson. 2011, Piatkus, London.

The Antidote: happiness for people who can't stand positive thinking, by Oliver Burkeman. 2012, Canongate Books Ltd, Edinburgh.

The Art of Happiness: a handbook for living, by HH Dalai Lama & Howard C. Cutler. 1998, Hodder and Stoughton, London.

Happiness by Design: finding pleasure and purpose in everyday life, by Paul Dolan. 2015, Penguin, London.

Rethinking Depression: how to shed mental health labels and create personal meaning, by Eric Maisel. 2012, New World Library, CA.

Moodmapping: plot your way to emotional health and happiness, by Dr Liz Miller. 2009, Rodale, London.

Illustrating Ideas

Venn That Tune, by Andrew Viner. 2008, Hodder & Stoughton Ltd, London.

Lifestyle Choices

The Moneyless Man: a year of freeconomic living, by Mark Boyle. 2010, Oneworld Publications, London.

The Case for Working with Your Hands: or why office work is bad for us and fixing things feels good, by Matthew Crawford. 2009, Penguin, London.

The North

The North: and almost everything in it, by Paul Morley. 2014, Bloomsbury Publishing, London.

Addiction

The Only Way to Stop Smoking Permanently, by Allen Carr. 1995, Penguin, London.

Memoirs of an Addicted Brain: a neuroscientist examines his former life on drugs, by Marc Lewis, Phd. 2012, Public Affairs, NY.

Love and Addiction, by Stanton Peele with Archie Brodsky. 1975, NAL Penguin, NY.

The Truth About Addiction and Recovery, by Stanton Peele and Archie Brodsky. 1992, Fireside, NY.

7 Tools to Beat Addiction, by Stanton Peele. 2004, Three Rivers Press, NY.

Philosophy, Psychology and Psychotherapy

Person-Centred Therapy: a revolutionary paradigm, by Jerold Bozarth. 1998, PCCS Books, Ross-on-Wye.

The Essential Dalai Lama, by HH the Dalai Lama. 2005, Hodder and Stoughton, London.

The Art of Being, by Erich Fromm. 1993, Constable & Robinson, London.

To Have or To Be, by Erich Fromm. 1997, Continuum, NY.

Emotional Intelligence: why it can matter more than IQ, by Daniel Goleman. 1996, Bloomsbury Publishing, London.

The Examined Life: how we lose and find ourselves, by Stephen Grosz. 2014, Vintage, London.

Buddhism: plain and simple, by Steve Hagan. 1999, Penguin, London.

I'm OK – You're OK, by Thomas A. Harris. 1973, Pan Books, London.

Minding What Matters: psychotherapy and the Buddha within, by Robert Langan. 2006, Wisdom Publications, MA.

Toward a Psychology of Being, by Abraham H. Maslow. 1962, D. Van Nostrand Company, NJ.

Invitation to Person-Centred Psychology, by Tony Merry. 2006, PCCS Books, Ross-on-Wye.

The Road Less Travelled, by M. Scott Peck. 1990, Arrow Books, London.

The Road Less Travelled and Beyond: spiritual growth in an age of anxiety, by M. Scott Peck. 1997, Simon & Schuster, NY.

Zen and the Art of Motorcycle Maintenance, by Robert. M. Pirsig. 1976, Corgi, London.

Client-Centred Therapy, by Carl R. Rogers. 2003, Constable and Robinson, London.

A Way of Being, by Carl R. Rogers. 1980, Houghton Mifflin, NY.

The Power of Now, by Eckhart Tolle. 2005, Hodder and Stoughton, London.